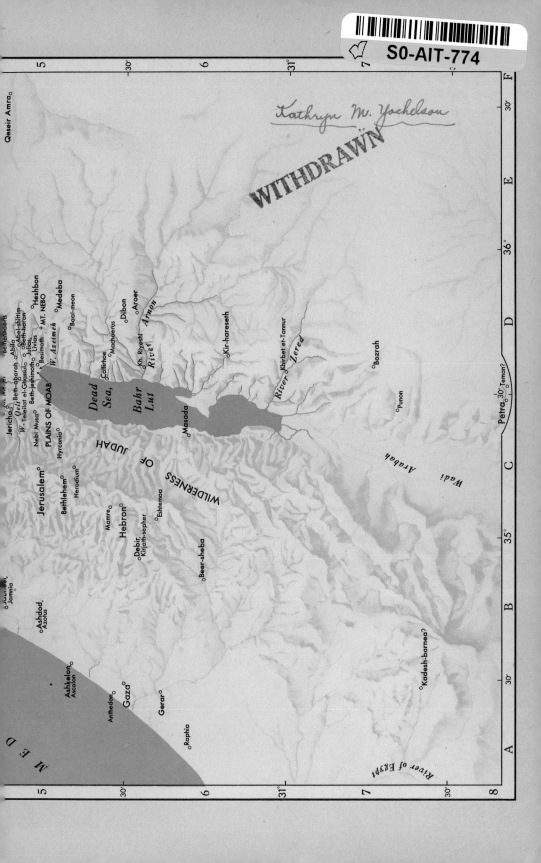

THE RIVER JORDAN

Photo by Keren Hayesod, Jerusalem

"The Jungle of the Jordan."

THE RIVER
JORDAN

Being an Illustrated Account of
Earth's Most Storied River

BY NELSON GLUECK

Director, American School of Oriental Research, Jerusalem

Field Director, American School of Oriental Research, Baghdad

Professor of Bible and Biblical Archaeology,
Hebrew Union College, Cincinnati

THE WESTMINSTER PRESS
PHILADELPHIA

PRINTED IN THE UNITED STATES OF AMERICA
THE LAKESIDE PRESS — R. R. DONNELLEY & SONS COMPANY
CHICAGO, ILLINOIS AND CRAWFORDSVILLE, INDIANA

To my wife

HELEN

at whose request this book

was written

Foreword

THIS *is an expression of wonder at the majesty of the Jordan. Who indeed can assemble and properly interpret all the factors that made for its importance? How can anyone adequately answer just why Judaism, Christianity, and their issue, Islam, developed along its banks and in adjacent lands? These are matters that can be contemplated and increasingly understood but not conclusively determined. And so it is that we study the Jordan with astonishment and awe, for there, to use the language of religious experience, miracles were made manifest.*

The fantastic river and its amazing valley, sunk in their incomparably deep trough, have left their mark on fifty thousand years and more of human history. This long story has been sketched in rapid strokes in these pages. Some persons, incidents, and sites have been highlighted to illustrate the whole. Many photographs have also been employed for this purpose. It is hoped that this outline will reveal something of the uniqueness and wonder of the Jordan, which is so centrally located in world geography and so vitally connected with much of the march of civilization.

The results of various discoveries concerning the ancient past of the Jordan Valley have been used, including the more recent ones obtained by the joint expedition of the American School of Oriental Research, Jerusalem, and The Smithsonian Institution, Washington, D. C.

Many have been of assistance in assembling material for this publication. I mention particularly Mr. A. S. Kirkbride, British Resident in Transjordan; el-Farik Glubb Pasha, Officer Commanding the Arab Legion in Transjordan; Mr. Lankester Harding, Chief Curator of Antiquities, Department of Antiquities, in Transjordan; Rashid Hamid, Subinspector, Department of Antiquities, in Transjordan; Mr. Robert Hamilton, Director of the Department of Antiquities in Palestine; and the following members of the Palestine Archaeological Museum: Mr. H. J. Iliffe, Curator; Mr. S. J. Schweig, Master Photographer, who is responsible for all the photographs in this book credited to the Palestine Department of Antiquities; Dr.

Emanuel Ben-Dor, Librarian; Mr. M. Avi-Yonah, Assistant Record Officer; and Dr.E. Henschel-Simon, Assistant Keeper.

Professors Millar Burrows, of Yale University, and William F. Albright, of Johns Hopkins University, respectively President and Vice-President of the American Schools of Oriental Research, have read this book in manuscript form, the latter going over it in great detail. It has benefited much from their criticisms and suggestions. Professor G. Ernest Wright, of McCormick Theological Seminary, has very kindly supervised the making of the maps, which are based on his earlier work, with his colleague, Floyd V. Filson, in The Westminster Historical Atlas to the Bible. *I am all the more grateful to Professors Wright and Albright, and to Rev. L. J. Trinterud, of The Westminster Press, for their editorial supervision, because it has been impossible for me while in Jerusalem to exercise any at all.*

NELSON GLUECK.

American School of Oriental Research,
Jerusalem,
March 26, 1945.

Contents

Illustrations

PAGE

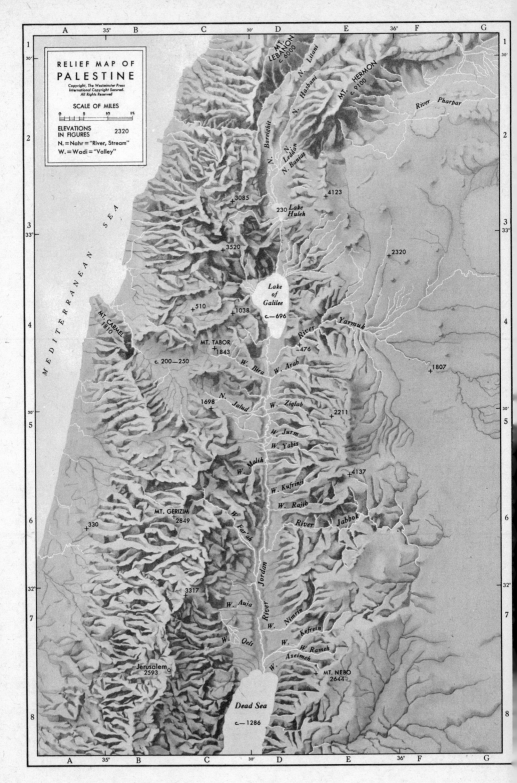

RELIEF MAP OF
PALESTINE
Copyright, The Westminster Press
International Copyright Secured.
All Rights Reserved

SCALE OF MILES
0   5   10   15

ELEVATIONS
IN FIGURES   2320
N. = Nahr = "River, Stream"
W. = Wadi = "Valley"

MEDITERRANEAN SEA

MT. LEBANON
c. 6000

N. Litani

N. Hasbani

MT. HERMON
c. 9100

River Pharpar

N. Bareighit

N. Leddan
N. Banias

+3085

230 Lake Huleh

+4123

+3520

+2320

Lake of Galilee
c. -696

+510

+1038

MT. CARMEL
1810

Yarmuk

River

MT. TABOR
+1843

-476

+1807

c. 200—250

W. Bira

W. Arab

N. Jalud
+1698

W. Ziglab

+2211

W. Jurm

W. Yabis

W. Malih

+4137

W. Kufrinji

W. Rajib

MT. GERIZIM
+2849

W. Far'ah

River   Jabbok

+330

+3317

W. Auja

River Jordan

W. Nimrin

W. Qelt

W. Kefrein
W. Rameh

W. Azeimeh

W.

Jerusalem
2593

MT. NEBO
2644

Dead Sea
c. -1286

2

I

The Jordan Rift

I

THE JORDAN is a weird stream (Fig. 1). It twists and tears its way swiftly downward in an almost incredibly sinuous manner from the sweet waters of the Lake of Galilee to the bitter wastes of the Sea of Salt or Dead Sea. Squirming frantically (Fig. 2), burrowing madly, seeking wildly to escape its fate, the Jordan's course from its crystal-clear beginnings to its literally dark and bitter end is a helpless race to a hopeless goal. Like Lot's wife, it looks backward, but only inevitably to perish in the perdition of *Bahr Lut*, the "Sea of Lot," as the Dead Sea is called by the Arabs (Fig. 3).

If a man from the moon were to look at the Jordan Valley, he would behold at first glance an apparently lunar landscape (Fig. 4). It would appear to him as part of a great crack in the crust of the earth, extending all the way from northern Syria south to the Red Sea. Were he gazing at the southern half of this fissure, which includes the Jordan Valley and its continuation, the Wadi Arabah or depression lying between the Dead Sea and the Gulf of Aqabah, he would see malevolent masses of gray chalky marl, fantastically cut hillocks, sands glittering with fool's gold, treacherously soft salty wastes, sandstone formations run riot with color, reddish brown ranges of haematite rock, black igneous mountains streaked with green. His glance would take in the leaden gray green of the Dead Sea and the dirty dark brown of the Jordan, relieved by the sparkling azure blue of the Lake of Galilee.

He would perceive perhaps that the floor of the great rift he was looking at rested on burning or cooling foundations. Boiling hot springs emerge along its surface. Quiescent volcanos and filled-in craters are visible. One of the craters contains the pond of Birket

Photo by The Matson Photo Service, Jerusalem

FIG. 1. The Jordan in its lower valley.

4

er-Ram (Lake Phiala), close to the Banias source of the Jordan. Earthquakes have destroyed cities in the Jordan Valley as large as Jericho, have caused landslides which dammed up the Jordan, and have shaken the threshold of the Temple in Jerusalem.

Indeed, earthquakes have been the *alter ego* of the ancient Near East. Certainly without them neither the Jordan nor the Nile Valley would have come into existence, because both of them were born probably from the same geological spasm. Several great upheavals blocked the thrust northward of the eastern arm of the Red Sea (the Gulf of Aqabah), which might otherwise have reached as far as Turkey partly through what is now the Jordan Valley. One upthrust fashioned the wall that helped to imprison the waters of the Jordan finally in a deep hole, the top of which is 1,286 feet below sea level, and the bottom of which is once again as deep. There, compounded with salts and sulphur and other chemicals drawn from the bowels of the earth, they were to form the witch's brew now known as the Dead Sea (Fig. 5).

2

In prehistoric times a life of tropical abundance flourished in the Jordan Valley. Let us transport ourselves in imagination to a moment of its distant past.

With mighty trampling down of reeds barring the way to the Jordan, some elephants burst through to the water's edge, waded into the river, and drank and played to their hearts' content. A bull elephant trumpeted loudly in lordly glee, and his *harîm* swished about with gargantuan gracefulness. The baby elephants cavorted with all the abandon of the young. After a while, at the leader's signal, the massive beasts, sides glistening wet and tusks gleaming white and wicked, moved ashore. There they browsed contentedly in the almost impenetrable thickets of the Jordan Valley, through which their hulks had hewn recognizable paths. Suddenly one of them crashed through the cunningly concealed cover of a deep pit, and hurtled down to be impaled on sharpened stakes. With shrill cackling and cries of content, there slouched from cover a band of hunters, who

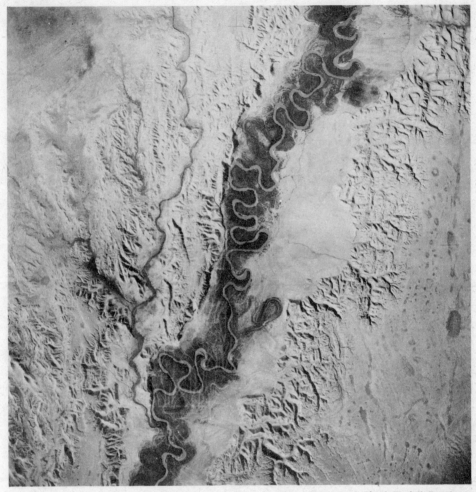

Fig. 2. The Jordan in its lush-green *Zor*, joined on the left by the Wadi Far'ah.

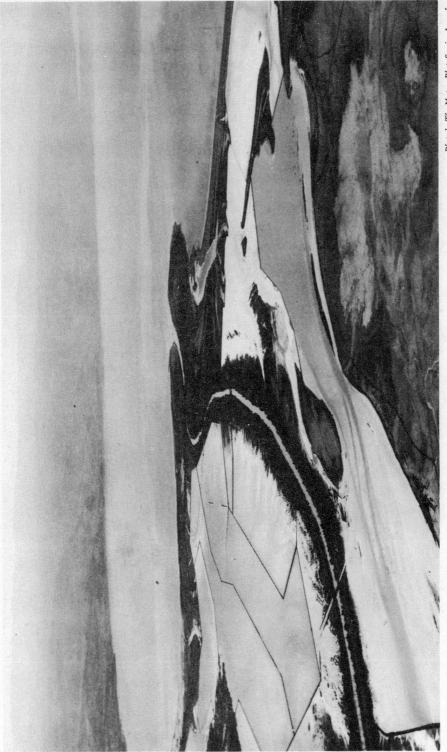

Fig. 3. The Jordan flowing through its delta into the Dead Sea.

7

FIG. 4. The Jordan winding through its Jungle, with moonlike hills extending between it and the upper part of the Jordan Valley.

FIG. 5. Salts pumped from the Dead Sea whiten evaporating pans straddling the Jordan near its mouth. Factories of the Palestine Potash, Ltd., are visible in the foreground, where potassium salts are processed. Bromine is a valuable by-product, among others including magnesium, chlorine, and sulphur.

FIG. 6. Prehistoric elephant's tusk from the Jordan Valley.

hacked at their thrashing victim with heavy axes and spears of flint and basalt, until finally it subsided in death.

This entire scene could have taken place and probably often did occur in prehistoric Palestine. Elephants roamed about, not only in the Jordan Valley, but also in the highlands and plains above and beyond them as far as the shores of the Mediterranean. Some of their skeletal remains and tusks have been found in caves near the eastern edge of the coastal plain; others in a garden on the highest point of Bethlehem, located in the hills a few miles from Jerusalem; and still others, together with flint and basalt axes, on the western bank of the Jordan, close by Jisr Banat Ya'qub, the "Bridge of the Daughters of Jacob," north of the Lake of Galilee. Indeed, among the remains dug up from the ancient bed of the Jordan was an elephant's tusk six feet long (Fig. 6).

The elephant hunters of the Jordan Valley were related to the prehistoric Galilee man, whose skull has been discovered near the Lake of Galilee (Fig. 7). Like their contemporaries elsewhere in the hills and plains of Palestine, they bagged other big game too, including rhinoceroses and hippopotamuses, as well as smaller animals. Palestine's prehistoric man was a mighty Nimrod. He belonged to a new species, which has become known as Paleoanthropus palestinensis. Skeletons found in caves near Mount Carmel, overlooking the Mediterranean, show a range from a Neanderthal type woman to a man with some strikingly modern characteristics. They lived perhaps a hundred thousand years ago. Ultimately they were replaced there, about 10,000 years ago, by the Natufian cave dwellers.

Prehistoric Palestine man lived as a hunter, usually in caves, employing tools and weapons of flint, basalt, and bone. The arts of agriculture, animal husbandry, architecture, metallurgy, pottery making, and weaving were unknown to him. He was blessed with few possessions. By the time of his very great Natufian grandchildren, however, the Modern Era had emerged. Its development was rapid and radical. People began in ever-increasing measure to plant and reap crops, raise animals, build houses, weave baskets, and dabble in art. Therewith ended the idyllic simplicity of the early ages. With these various activities, so far as our present knowledge goes, began the turbulent history of civilization in the Jordan Valley and the rest of Palestine. Its account has been volcanic ever since.

The change in the kind of men and women who peopled early Palestine may be correlated with important changes in climate. The gamut of change there in the period of the last 100,000 years extends from a damp and tropical climate when rhinoceroses, hippopotamuses, and elephants were plentiful to a dry, warm climate at the beginning of the Mesolithic Natufian period about 10,000 years ago, when gazelles and deer became abundant. From that day to this, there seem to have been no major, permanent, climatic changes in Palestine or the Near East, or probably anywhere on earth. It is known that since then deserts have appeared in great stretches of the world where fertile fields once abounded; that streams, rivers, and lakes have vanished, leaving nothing but dry beds in their place; and that great populations have perished where once multitudes flourished. These changes during the last ten millenniums have popularly been ascribed to changes in climate. Wherever it has been possible to check, it has been determined that they must be ascribed rather to factors over which there is a large measure of human control. They belong to the history of the work of man, as it can be told from about 10,000 years ago until now. In that history the happenings along the Jordan River have played an important role.

3

The fairest part of the great geological fault to which the Jordan Valley belongs is the Valley of the Lebanon. That is the literal translation of *Biq'ath ha-Lebanon*, as it is called in the Bible (Josh. 11:17). Hemmed in by the cypress- and cedar-adorned Lebanon Mountains on the west side, and by the Anti-Lebanon range on the east, the valley was once called "Hollow Syria" (Coele Syria), a name loosely applied at times to all of southern Syria and Palestine with the exception of Phoenicia. Its fertile fields and strong streams have helped to fill it with cities and settlements from earliest antiquity on. Their glittering crown was Baalbek.

Its founding fathers worshiped the god of fertility there. Baal was his name. The Greeks, however, had another word for it. They identified him with their sun-god, Helios. Baalbek was renamed Heliopolis, only to revert to its former name after the Greek sun had set. The Romans erected mighty temples there to some of their many gods. Byzantines changed these buildings into churches and basilicas, and Moslems into citadels and mosques. Mongols destroyed and massacred; earthquakes too had their disastrous innings; but the ruins still stand in imposing majesty. Six of the mighty columns of the Temple of Jupiter, each 62 feet high, and measuring seven and a half feet in diameter, hold themselves proudly erect to this very day. Their glorious Corinthian capitals command a distant view over the watered greenness of their valley (Fig. 8).

North of Baalbek, which stands on a watershed, at an elevation of some 3,600 feet, the Orontes (Nahr el-'Asi) sets its course, finally to flow by the city of Antioch at a point about 20 miles from its outlet into the Mediterranean Sea. The evangelical efforts of early Christianity proved most fruitful at Antioch. There "Saul who is also called Paul" and Barnabas established the central Church, to which they would return at journey's end (Acts 11:19–26; 13:1–3, 14; 14:26). It was at Antioch by the Orontes that the converts to the new faith which was preached with such Jewish passion by Paul and Barnabas were first called "Christians" (Acts 11:26).

4

To the south of Baalbek the union of four streams creates the river that is well named the Jordan, that is, the "River That Goes Down." Called *esh-Sheria*, the "Drinking Place," by the Arabs, it journeys downward, ever downward, from the glittering snows of Mount Hermon, which perpetually cap its top, to the turbid depths of the Dead Sea. Washed white with snow at its beginnings, it soon acquires a muddy coloring. Finally, it flings its silt far into the sea's salty waters before being swallowed alive, as were the sites of Sodom and Gomorrah.

High above the beginnings of the Jordan stands Mount Hermon

©N. G. S. Photo by Maynard Owen Williams. Reproduced by special permission of The National Geographic Magazine

Fig. 7. In this cave, overlooking the Lake of Galilee, was found the skull of a prehistoric man who lived perhaps 100,000 years ago.

FIG. 8. Mount Lebanon is seen through six columns of Jupiter's temple; a broken pillar leans against Bacchus' shrine at Baalbek. The lintels and stones of modern houses in left foreground were taken from the Roman ruins.

Photo by The Matson Photo Service, Jerusalem

FIG. 9. Snow-clad Mount Hermon seen from River Barbar (Pharpar) east of it.

(Fig. 9), its hoary head lending it grave and beautiful distinction. The *Jebel esh-Sheikh*, the "Mountain Chieftain," as it is called by the Arabs, dominates the entire Jordan Valley. The Targums, Aramaic translations of the Bible, knew it as the *Tur Talga*, the "Mountain of Snow." Walking in the Jordan Valley on a torrid summer day, at a point not far north of Jericho, I have glimpsed from afar the gleam of its quiet coolness (Fig. 10). Its whiteness is reflected in the waters of the Lake of Galilee, whose very existence depends chiefly upon its bounty.

The mountain range of Hermon extends from northeast to southwest for a distance of nearly twenty miles. Its principal peak, resembling an immense truncated cone, is divided into three summits, the highest of which towers 9,101 feet high, with the other two only a little lower. No wonder then that this stalwart sentinel was anciently dedicated to divinity, and made the seat of gods. The temple of the chief of them, Baal-hermon (Judg. 3:3), graced its top, and shrines were strewn around its base, where the melting snow appeared in unceasing springs and full-born streams. "As far as Mount Hermon" was a phrase full of meaning to multitudes whose lives were influenced by its fonts, to travelers whose eyes were bent toward the familiar landmark, to armies for which it was variously a bulwark and a barrier. Many nations knew it, some by other names. The Bible tells us that Mount Hermon was called Sirion by the Sidonians, while the Amorites called it Senir (Deut. 3:9). And the psalmist prayed when disquieted: "O my God, my soul is cast down within me: Therefore am I mindful of thee from the land of the Jordan, and the Hermons" (Ps. 42:6).

5

The easternmost of the sources of the Jordan is the Nahr Banias, which is born at the base of Mount Hermon. It is only about five and a half miles long, but the manner of its origin has forced men from early times on to pause and ponder upon the mystery of creation. The traveler crosses a small, deep gorge through which the stream forces its way. Continuing upward, one sees that it issues from a flat, boulder-strewn area of considerable size, filled with brush, fern, oleander, grass, and flowers in season. Among them gurgle and frolic numerous small streams, which split apart and join together in an endless game. To anyone acquainted with the arid Near East, where water is worth its weight in gold and more to be prized than precious jewels, the sight of all this wealth of water gladdens the heart. The impulse of the observer is to break into a little dance, and to exclaim with his Arab companion, "*Ma sh'allah,*" which is the equivalent, in this instance, of "How wonderful!" His amazement and elation grow apace as he advances to the very beginnings of this bountiful blessing. A great, precipitous, iron-reddened, limestone cliff looms up. In it is a large cave, earthquake-battered. From its base there bursts forth a full-formed stream, that seems to shout as it emerges, "Get out of my way, for here I come." Like a lively lad, it plunges into play, rushing about wildly and singing at the top of its voice. The sweet melody can be heard from afar. Man's natural reaction, when confronted with this amazing and happy manifestation of new life, is to be lost in awe.

Throughout the ages men have built shrines and temples by this spot, and celebrated joyous festivals in near-by groves. The ancient Baals were worshiped with pagan naturalness. Was this perhaps the seat of "Baal-gad in the valley of the Lebanon" (Josh. 12:7)? And what was more natural for the Greeks to do when they first arrived than to dedicate the cave to their vigorous and lustful god, Pan, and to his playmates, the nymphs? No more appropriate place could be imagined for him, where he could skip and leap with heathenish abandon. They carved his name together with that of the nymphs in the first line of a Greek inscription on the rock of the cave: *PANI TE KAI NYMPHAIS.* They gave the name of Paneion to the place, and called the town and district Paneas. The latter is the name that has endured to this day. The Arabs call it Banias, because every *p* becomes a *b* in their pronunciation.

The name Paneas was changed several times, but none of the new names stuck. The part-Idumaean and part-Jew Herod the Great received the whole district as a present from Augustus. He attempted

FIG. 10. Lake of Galilee, with Mount Hermon reflected in it.

FIG. 11. Herod the Great's massive port of Caesarea, on the Mediterranean coast of Palestine, is represented today by remains of broken piers and numerous fallen columns.

FIG. 12. The cliff at Banias (Paneas, Caesarea Philippi), with its Pan niches, marking the worship of Pan at the point whence the waters issue at the base of the cliff to form the Nahr Banias, the easternmost of the sources of the Jordan. On the top of the cliff at the left stands the Mohammedan shrine of Sheikh Khudr, or St. George, who is venerated in Moslem as well as Christian tradition. It may mark the site of the temple erected by Herod the Great in honor of Augustus.

FIG. 13. The Pan niche cut in the face of the cliff at Banias above an artificially hewn cave. Under the niche is a Greek inscription commemorating the god Pan.

FIG. 14. 'Ain Leddan, by Tell el-Qadi (ancient Dan), forming one of the main sources of the Jordan.

to show his appreciation by building in honor of his patron a temple of white marble, placed probably on top of the cliff. Herod's son, Philip, established his residence in Paneas, and called the town Caesarea. It became known as Caesarea Philippi (i.e., Philip's Caesarea), to distinguish it from his father's Caesarea on the Mediterranean coast of Palestine (Fig. 11).

Destroyed and rebuilt by Agrippa II, the town was renamed by him Neronias, in honor of Nero. Among the coins of the town may be seen one with the laureled head of Apollo on one side and the figure of Poppaea, Nero's wife, visible inside a pillared temple, on the other. The brutal emperor first kicked his wife to death, and then had her proclaimed a goddess.

The odor of pagan sanctity hovered long about Paneas. Eusebius tells us of some of the rites practiced there in the fourth century of our era. His account reads: "At Caesarea Philippi, which the Phoenicians call Paneas, springs are shown at the foot of the Mountain Panius, out of which the Jordan flows. They say that on a certain feast day a victim was thrown in, and that through the power of the demon it marvelously disappeared and that which happened was a famous wonder to those who were present. Astyrius was once there when these things were done, and seeing the multitudes astonished at the affair, he pitied their delusion; and looking up to heaven he supplicated the God over all through Christ that he would rebuke the demon who deceived the people, and bring the men's delusion to an end. And they say that when he had prayed thus, immediately the sacrifice floated on the surface of the fountain. And thus the miracle departed; and no wonder was ever afterward performed at the place."[1] Today, on top of the cliff of Paneion, on whose side Pan niches can still be seen (Figs. 12, 13), stands the Mohammedan shrine of Sheikh Khudr, or Saint George, who is venerated in Moslem as well as Christian tradition. It seems to say, "Like the Roman temple that preceded me, I, too, testify to the fact that this is holy ground."

One day there came to Banias, then known as Caesarea Philippi, a

---

[1] Nicene and Post-Nicene Fathers, 2d series, Vol. I, *The Church History of Eusebius,* VII:17. Ed. Schaff, P., and Wace, H. New York, 1890.

Jew named Jesus and his disciples. The little band of Semites must have looked with astonishment at the shrines and temples and palaces with which the source of the river and the site of the town were adorned. Slight of figure, bearded and bronzed, they must have drawn their simple cloaks more tightly around them in a gesture of dismay. Jesus was as conscious of beauty as any of his fellow men, but surely this was blasphemy! God could not be found in buildings or groves by fountains unless the worshipers cast all evil from their hearts, removed deceptive symbols from their shrines, and practiced deeds of righteousness hallowed by the consciousness of the beauty of holiness. God could not be caught in blocks of marble, nor figured with the features of mortal men. As Jesus looked about him in the vainglorious city standing by this source of the Jordan, could not he, familiar as he was with the teachings of Jeremiah, have been recalling these words: "Are there among the vanities of the nations any that have the power to cause rain? or doth the heaven give showers? art thou not he, O Lord our God? In thee do we hope: for thou hast made all these things" (Jer. 14:22)?

Jesus was of the spiritual stock of Jeremiah, who spoke in the name of God: "Circumcise yourselves to the Lord; remove the foreskin from your hearts" (Jer. 4:4). In this sense, the words of Paul uttered in accordance with the Gospel of Jesus might have been spoken to the Jews of Jerusalem or to those who dwelt in Caesarea Philippi: "For he is not a Jew who is one outwardly. Neither is that a circumcision which is outward in the flesh. But he is a Jew who is one inwardly; whose praise is not of men, but of God. Circumcision is that of the heart; in the spirit, and not in the letter" (Rom. 2:28, 29). Jesus was also of the same prophetic background as Amos, who had said: "The Lord hath spoken. Who can but prophesy?" (Amos 3:8). And it is in the light of this background that the utterance of Jesus at Caesarea Philippi might well be considered: "Now when Jesus came into the parts of Caesarea Philippi, he asked his disciples, saying, Who do men say that the Son of man is? And they replied, Some say John the Baptist; some say Elijah; and others, Jeremiah, or one of the prophets. . . . And Simon Peter answered and said unto

Photo by Govt. of Palestine, Dept. of Antiquities

FIG. 14a. Looking north at the long, low, tree- and bush-covered mound of el-Qadi, the Biblical Dan, marking the northern of the two cities of Dan and Beersheba, which delimited, respectively, the northern and southern extent of ancient Palestine.

FIG. 15. Et-Tannur, place of a waterfall in the Nahr Bareighit, the westernmost of the sources of the Jordan.

FIG. 16. Nahr Bareighit, one of the sources of the Jordan.

him, Thou art the Christ, the Son of the living God" (Matt. 16: 13–16).

That marked a turning point in the life of Jesus. He decided then to go back to Jerusalem, knowing that he might suffer because of his quarrel with unrighteous elders and scribes and priests, and be killed by Romans because of his allegedly revolutionary activity against their regime. His was the exalted tradition of the great prophets. Hosea had declared in the name of God, "Love do I desire, and not sacrifices; and knowledge of God, not holocausts" (Hos. 6:6). Isaiah, among others, had inveighed against exaggerated and senseless ritual, and cried out in the name of God to his people: "Cleanse and purify yourselves. Remove your wicked deeds from mine eyes. Cease to do evil; learn to do good. Practice justice. Hold in check the oppressor. Secure the right of the fatherless. Plead the cause of the widow" (Isa. 1:16, 17). None of these men were afraid of consequences; nor was Jesus. When Peter attempted to restrain him from following his decision made at Caesarea Philippi, he turned upon Peter and said, "Get thee behind me, Satan: thou art a stumbling-block unto me: for thou mindest not the things of God, but the things of men" (Matt. 16:23).

6

A forty-minute walk west of Banias brings one to another out-burst of underground water. The strong springs of 'Ain Leddan (Fig. 14) fill two large dips in the ground with swirling pools of water. Located west and southwest of the great artificial city-mound of Tell el-Qadi (Fig. 14a), they spill into a stream that flows like a freshet to form the shortest but strongest source of the Jordan. It is known as the Nahr el-Leddan. Its name reflects that of the tribe of Dan, which conquered the ancient Phoenician-controlled city of Laish (Leshem), now identified with Tell el-Qadi, and gave it the name of Dan (Judg. 18:27; Josh. 19:47). The Arabic *Qadi* and the Hebrew *Dan* both mean "Judge," so that it would be possible to speak of the "City of the Judge" located by the Spring and River of the Judge. It stood on the northern border of ancient Israel, and marks today the boundary be-

tween Palestine and Syria. The phrase, "From Dan . . . to Beer-sheba"
(I Sam. 3:20), became a household word. It is supposed to have been
quoted by the Bible-bred Welshman, Lloyd George, before a boundary commission at the Versailles Conference in 1919, when he insisted that the territory of modern Palestine had to extend as far
north as the site of ancient Dan.

7

The longest source of the Jordan, and the one most directly in line
with it, is the Nahr Hasbani. It is about 24 miles long. Starting from
an excellent spring at the foot of one of the buttresses of Mount
Hermon, it parallels for a considerable distance the lower part of the
southern course of the Leontes. The two streams are separated less
than 5 miles from each other, until the Leontes (Nahr el-Litani) turns
westward toward the Mediterranean, into which it empties.

The westernmost source of the Jordan is the small mountain
stream, Nahr Bareighit (Figs. 15, 16). Through a rude gorge, it
tumbles down southward from the hilly meadowland of Merj 'Ayun,
which retains in clear part its ancient Biblical name of Ijon (I Kings
15:20), to add its waters to the formation of the fateful river. The
Nahr Bareighit joins the Nahr Hasbani about three quarters of a mile
above the point where the Hasbani joins the junction of the Leddan
and Banias streams. These last two alone were anciently considered
as the sole sources of the Jordan. All four help to form it, and lose
their identity in it, as the Jordan starts its flow under its own name.

> "Roll, Jordan, roll;
> I want to go to heaven when I die
> To hear sweet Jordan roll."

Fig. 17. Tell Abil, the site of Biblical Abel-beth-maachah, on the east side of the Nahr Bareighit, overlooking the marshlands of Huleh from an elevation above their northwest end.

31

Photo by Govt. of Palestine, Dept. of Antiquities

FIG. 18. Looking southeast at Tell Abil (Abel-beth-maachah), with part of the partly drained and cultivated marshlands of Huleh visible below it. On top of Tell Abil is the modern Arab village of Abel el-Qamh.

II

The Lake District

I

THE JORDAN commences its journey as a river in its own right by passing through the lands of Huleh (Figs.17, 18). The water table is very near the surface there, and the complete absence of drainage canals makes for the creation of a large swamp or group of swamps. There are numerous springs. Water buffalo wallow about, and are today employed to help in planting rice and in plowing the existing small stretches of dry land. Reeds, bulrushes, and high grass flourish. Papyrus plants thrive. It is possible that from them was made some of the papyrus which served as paper in antiquity. Jackals, hyenas, and boars abound. All manner of birds and waterfowl can be seen. It is low and hot and feverish in the Huleh region, whose waters are gathered into the small Lake Huleh at its southern end. Practically all the Arab children born in the swamps in the spring and summer months die in early infancy of malaria. Their elders are worn with the ravages of this disease, which they believe comes from the "hot air." The hills, rising on the east and west to a height of about 3,000 feet, are still far below the height of Mount Hermon, coolly oblivious of its surroundings.

Overlooking the Huleh area from an elevation above its northwest end is the great mound of Tell Abil (Figs. 17, 18), the Biblical Abel-beth-maachah. It was once besieged by Joab, David's general, because Sheba, the son of Bichri, a Benjamite, had fled there after leading a vain revolt against David. Joab's siege of the city was lifted when a woman residing there promised to deliver Sheba's head to him if he undertook to do the city no further harm. "Then she went and advised all the people [of Abel-beth-maachah] in her wisdom. And they cut off the head of Sheba, the son of Bichri, and

33

FIG. 19. Sea-level sign, using the Mediterranean's surface as the gauge. The sign is repeated in the three official languages of Palestine. The English "Sea Level" is translated below it into the Arabic "Roof of the Sea" at the left and Hebrew "Face of the Sea" at the right. The Lake of Galilee is 696 feet below this point.

34

threw it down to Joab. So he blew the trumpet, and they were dispersed from the city, each to his home. And Joab returned to Jerusalem to the king" (II Sam. 20:21, 22).

2

After a flow of little less than 7 miles, the newly formed Jordan empties into Lake Huleh, which Josephus knew as Lake Semechonitis. It is triangularly shaped, being some 3 miles long and over 2 wide at its upper end and narrowing down to a point at its southern end. It varies from about 9 to 16 feet in depth.

Gathering increased strength from this large pocket of water, the Jordan leaves Lake Huleh quietly enough and holds itself in to a fairly steady pace for about 2 miles. Then, just beyond Jisr Banat Ya'qub, the "Bridge of the Daughters of Jacob," over which leads the highroad between Damascus and Galilee, it tears out on a run that, for some distance, brooks no restraint. It tumbles and cascades almost continuously through a forbidding, black basalt gorge. Foaming and muddy, it bursts out of the ravine. Then, collecting itself somewhat, it wriggles its way for about another mile through a small plain and a delta of its own making into the clear waters of the Lake of Galilee. In the distance of about 10 miles between the two lakes, the river plunges from 230 feet above sea level to 696 feet below (Fig. 19).

3

The Lake of Galilee is visible in wonderful perspective from the heights of the Qurun Hattin, the Horns of Hattin, which tower almost 2,000 feet above it to the west. They form the top of an extinct volcano, which is quite in place among the broad black deposits of basalt on the eastern side of the hills of Galilee. There, on the waterless heights of Hattin, was fought a frightful battle between the Crusaders and the Moslems. It raged from July 2 to July 4, 1187. On the last day, the Christian army could no longer withstand the attack of Saladin's soldiery. To the burning heat of the sun and the blinding, choking dust raised by the battle was added the scorching

southerly wind of a khamsin, blowing from the desert. In addition
there was a fearful lack of water. In the valley below, but a few scanty
miles away, could be seen the sparkling blue of the Lake of Galilee.
The knights and troops drawn from the fairest lands of Europe had
frequently bathed in it, and its cool waters had often quenched their
thirst. To the north the smaller patch representing the Lake of Huleh
could be made out. The dark line between them was the track of the
Jordan. Now it was all become nothing more than a miserable
mirage, tantalizingly near, tormenting the pilgrim warriors. How
could men fight and human flesh endure when throats were choked
with dust, and lips were cracked wide open, and limbs were leadened
beyond the power to move them, all for lack of water? A few of the
Crusaders escaped, but most of them were cut down relentlessly by
the very men whom they themselves would otherwise have put to the
sword. "A militant and truculent Christianity, as false as the relics of
the 'True Cross' round which it was rallied, met its judicial end
within view of the scenes where Christ proclaimed the Gospel of
Peace, and went about doing good."[1]

Standing on the shore of the Lake of Galilee one day, I heard a
distant humming in the sky, which soon grew to a steady roar. Suddenly, out of the sun flew a mighty seaplane to circle and settle on the
surface of the lake (Fig. 20). A tug put out from Tiberias to fetch its
passengers. Almost two thousand years have intervened since the
little boat in which Jesus and his disciples were seated was tossed
about dangerously by one of the sudden tempests that beat the normally calm waters into a raging fury. To his worried disciples Jesus
had said, "Why are ye fearful, O ye of little faith?" (Matt. 8:26). The
storm died down, and their boat made port safely. Much has been
changed since then; but the contours and character of the lake itself
remain as they were. Thirteen miles long, and about 8 miles across at
its greatest width, it is shaped like a harp, perhaps thereby receiving
its ancient name of Chinnereth. Its waters are clear and sweet, and at
one point over 150 feet deep. Not only the Jordan, but numerous,
strong underground streams feed it. One can swim along its shores

[1] Smith, George Adam, *The Historical Geography of the Holy Land* (25th ed.), p. 441.

Fig. 20. The flying boat *Satyrus* on the Lake of Galilee.

Photo by The Maison Photo Service, Jerusalem

FIG. 21. Modern Jewish settlement of Dagania in foreground, and Arabic village of Samakh in background, on south shore of Lake of Galilee.

FIG. 22. Modern Tiberias, Lake of Galilee, and Mount Hermon in the distance.

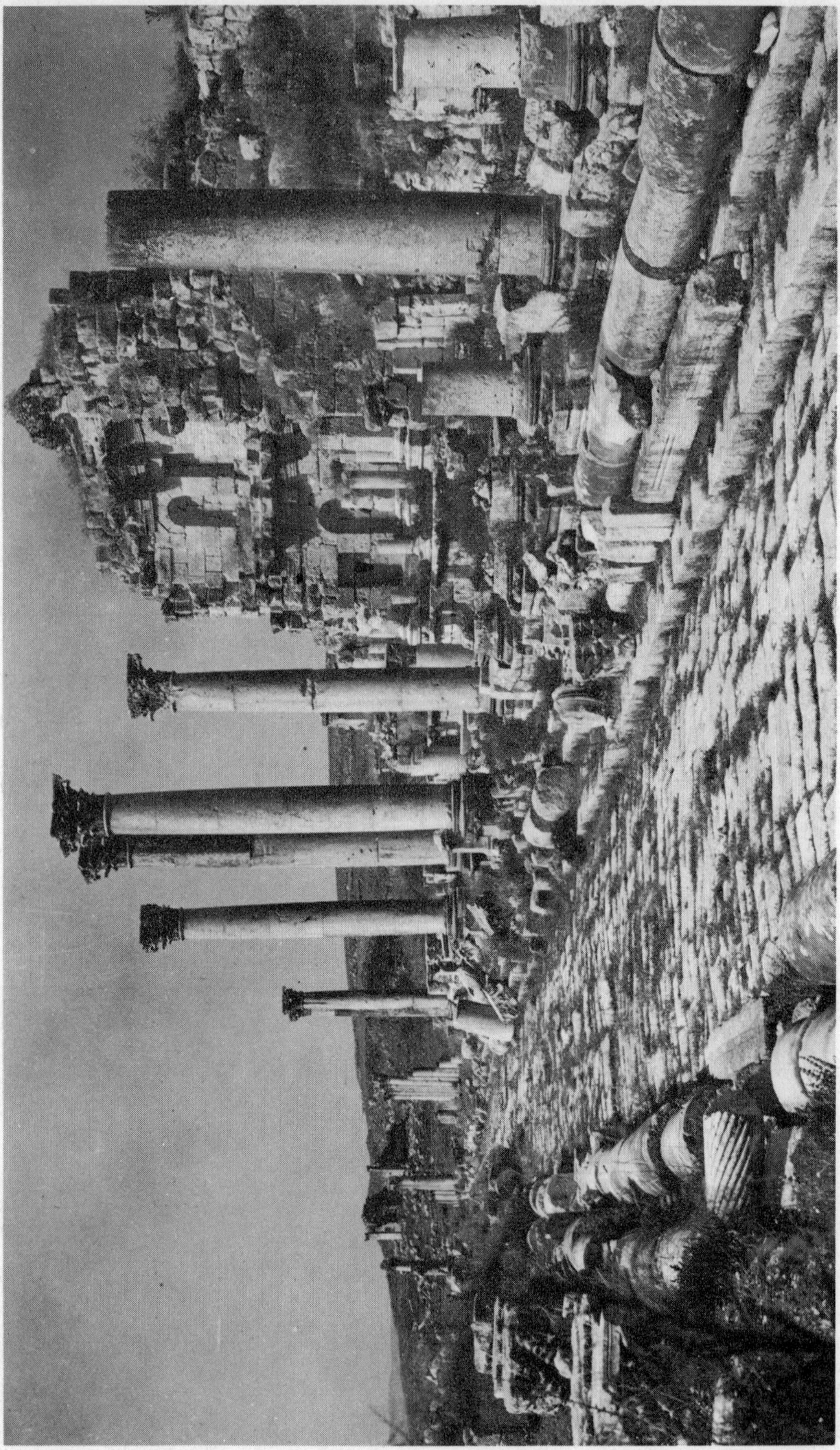

FIG. 23. Main thoroughfare of Roman Gerasa, Transjordan.

in warm waters, and suddenly be plunged into an icy bath when passing through the area over an upsurging cold spring. It is still full of fish. Hugged by the high hills of Galilee to the west and of the Jaulan to the east, it has only a narrow coast. This spreads out for a distance of less than 4 miles in the Ghuweir, the "Little Valley," along its northwest shore, which is to be identified with the land of Gennesaret.

The lava-fed fertility of the shores of the lake easily supports a rich tropical vegetation. Numerous springs supply much water for irrigation. Newly settled Jewish colonies are reviving agricultural activity on an intensive scale around the lake (Fig. 21). The barrenness and desolation which, until recently, many a pious pilgrim thought to be a part of historic patrimony would have been completely unfamiliar to Jesus. He and his disciples traveled to and fro across the much-used lake, near which so important a part of his life was spent. A belt of plantations then girdled its shores, forming the setting for some of the fairest towns of the Hellenistic-Roman Near East. There were 9 of these towns around the lake. Temples and synagogues, palaces and hippodromes, theaters and bathhouses, all done in the Greek manner, set off this carefully cultivated paradise. Industry thrived. The sound of the carpenter's hammer was a common one. Hardy fishermen brought home great catches of fish, which in part were dried and exported beyond the reaches of Palestine. Net weaving, hide tanning, and boatbuilding were among other familiar trades. Fruits and vegetables and other crops were produced in great quantity.

Listen to the words of Josephus, a Jewish nobleman who governed Galilee a little over a generation after the time of Jesus: "Now this lake of Gennesareth is so called from the country adjoining to it. . . . Its waters are sweet, and very agreeable for drinking. . . . The lake is also pure, and . . . of a temperate nature when you draw it up . . . . There are several kinds of fish in it. . . . The country also that lies over against this lake hath the same name of Gennesareth. . . . its soil is so fruitful that all sorts of trees can grow upon it. . . . One may call this place the ambition of nature" (*The Jewish War*, III: x. 7, 8).

4

The power of Rome was paraded around the Lake of Galilee. The somber city of Tiberias was its main stronghold there (Fig. 22). It was peopled at first with society's castoffs, and was long shunned by the Jews, because, when laying the foundations, its builders had disturbed an ancient necropolis. However, the nearness of hot mineral baths to the city lent growing attractiveness to it. After the destruction of Jerusalem by the Romans, it became a Jewish cultural center. The Palestine or Jerusalem Talmud was completed, and the Tiberian system of Hebrew punctuation developed there. The black ruins of the Roman acropolis which protected the city can still be seen above it. The natural strength of the location of Tiberias helped to preserve it as an occupied site down to this day, although it has perhaps the least attractive position of any along the entire lake. It is situated on the narrowest part of the coast, with little green available to relieve its grimness. The fine breezes that blow from the west during the summer do not favor it. Did Jesus shun the place, or is it just an accident that it is not mentioned in the Gospels? The Roman troops stationed there were probably frequently moved for relief from its humid heat to camps and cities in the hills above. Indeed, Roman legions, sometimes heavy-handed, dominated the life of the times. The prevalent architecture and the most pretentious religious expression were also Roman. Is it to be wondered at that the madman whose oppressed spirit Jesus healed called himself by the commonly repeated name of Legion? "And he [Jesus] asked him, What is thy name? And he said unto him, My name is Legion" (Mark 5:9).

Chief among the neighboring Roman hill towns was Gadara, dominating the heights on the east side of the Jordan, and overlooking the Yarmuk from the south. It commanded a wonderful view over the Lake of Galilee and the approaches to it from the southeast. It does not take much imagination for the modern visitor to visualize Gadara in its heyday. The remains of three theaters, a temple, a magnificent colonnaded street, a large reservoir and an aqueduct, give kindling idea of its former grandeur. The ruins of a later basilica can

FIG. 24. Looking north from Temple of Zeus, across Forum, and down main thoroughfare of Roman Gerasa, Transjordan.

FIG. 25. South Theater and Forum in Roman Gerasa, Transjordan.

FIG. 26. Temple of Artemis in Gerasa, Transjordan. Jesus saw temples such as this when he visited Caesarea Philippi by the Paneas source of the Jordan.

45

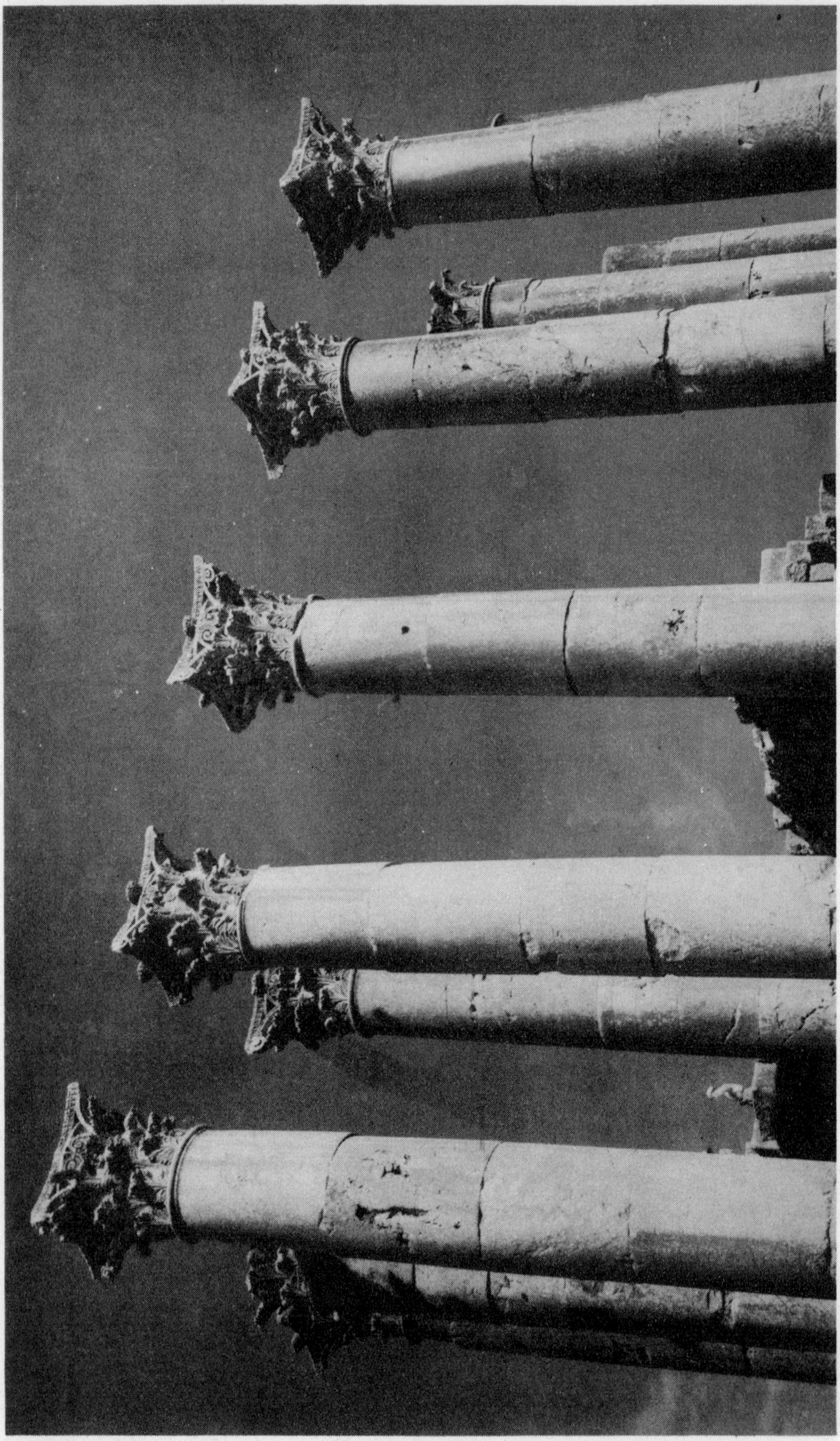

FIG. 27. Temple of Artemis, Gerasa. Detail of columns.

FIG. 28. Temple of Artemis, Gerasa. Detail of capitals.

47

also be made out. Some of the Roman and Byzantine remains have been built into the mean houses of the modern Arab village of Umm Qeis at the east end of the site. Like its sister city of Gerasa in Transjordan, whose ruins are much better preserved (Figs. 23, 24, 25, 26, 27, 28), Gadara belonged to the cities of the Decapolis, which were an adornment to Roman dominion. The name of Gadara is best remembered today in connection with the story of the Gadarene swine: "And when he [Jesus] was come to the other side into the country of the Gadarenes, there met him two possessed with demons. . . . They cried out, What have we to do with thee, thou Son of God? . . . And the demons besought him, saying, If thou cast us out, send us away into the herd of swine. . . . And, behold, the whole herd rushed down the steep into the sea [of Galilee], and perished in the waters" (Matt. 8:28–32).

Far below Gadara, on the north side of the Yarmuk River at the bottom of the gorge, are what may well be the finest hot springs of the entire Near East. Of old, from near and far, people sought out their curative waters. An ancient mound at el-Hammeh, the "Hot Springs," as the site is known today, testifies to the presence there of a settlement as early as the fourth millennium before the time of Christ (Fig. 29). It was called *Hamath Geder* in the Talmud. I have made soundings there, and can testify to the high material culture of its early inhabitants, as illustrated by the pottery they made. It may perhaps be these very springs, close to the Jordan, that figure in the story of the Syrian leper, Naaman, captain of the host of the king of Syria. He "dipped himself seven times in the Jordan, according to the saying of [Elisha] the man of God: and his flesh came again like unto the flesh of a little child, and he was clean" (II Kings 5:14). I shall never forget one day, while bathing there myself, suddenly seeing a leper slip into the far end of the pool I was in. Needless to say, I got out in a hurry.

The Romans built magnificent bathhouses at el-Hammeh, with a complicated system of underground channels. They also erected a theater there. These celebrated hot springs and baths of Amatha, as the Romans called the place, are mentioned, together with Gadara, by Strabo: "To Gadara the pleasure-loving Romans, after having enjoyed the restorative effects of the hot springs, retired for refreshment, enjoying the cooler heights of the city and solacing their leisure with the plays performed in the theaters." The remains of a fine synagogue of the Byzantine period have been discovered at el-Hammeh. This synagogue is related to the one at Gerasa, where scenes of the Flood story are depicted on a mosaic floor (Fig. 30). A basalt block recovered from Gadara, with a menorah, or candelabrum, carved on it, indicates the presence of a synagogue there also.

Over 30 synagogues belonging to the Roman and Byzantine periods have thus far been discovered in Palestine and Transjordan, most of them in Galilee. It seems inevitable that many more will be found. In the Jordan Valley, we already know one at 'Ain Duk, the Biblical Naaran, several miles northwest of Jericho, and another near ancient Jericho, discovered while land was being prepared for a banana plantation. The 'Ain Duk synagogue, which dates to the fifth century A.D., had a colorful mosaic floor of a type found commonly in Byzantine synagogues. There were also Aramaic inscriptions commemorating the donors and builders of the mosaics. One of the mosaic panels at 'Ain Duk depicted twelve signs of the zodiac, with their Hebrew names, in a circle around the sun chariot. Another showed the figure of Daniel, approached by two lions, with the words in Hebrew, "Daniel, peace." A third panel consisted of linked polygons, circles and semicircles, which served as frames for pictures of animals, birds, and plants. A fourth contained a picture of the ark of the Torah, flanked by a seven-branched candlestick on each side, with two glass lamps hanging from each candlestick.

The Byzantine synagogue near Tell es-Sultan at Jericho was oriented toward Jerusalem, and was built in the form of a basilica, with a central nave and two lateral aisles. These features are common to all the ancient synagogues thus far discovered in Palestine. It has a highly decorated mosaic floor, whose tesserae are white, red, black, brown, and blue. At one end is an Aramaic inscription, which is dedicated to those whose gifts made the mosaic floor possible. In the middle of the floor is a circular panel, with a seven-branched candle-

FIG. 29. The Yarmuk River. In the middle of the bend stands the ancient artificial city mound of el-Hammeh.

FIG. 30. Part of Flood story in mosaic floor of Byzantine synagogue
at Jerash (Gerasa), Transjordan.

Photo by Govt. of Palestine, Dept. of Antiquities

FIG. 31. Mosaic floor of Byzantine synagogue
at Tell es-Sultan, Jericho.

stick (menorah), a palm branch (lulab) on its left, and a ram's horn (shofar) on its right. Beneath it is an inscription in Aramaic characters, reading, "Peace be upon all Israel." Above this mosaic medallion is a representation of the Torah shrine (Fig. 31). All these synagogues were a powerful factor in the perpetuation of the basic principles of Judaism, as expounded by such great teachers as Rabbi Hillel.

5

About three miles southwest of the place where the Upper Jordan empties into the Lake of Galilee lies Capernaum, called in Aramaic Kefar Nahum (the Village of Nahum), now known as Tell Hum. It is situated close to the shore, at the edge of the rich plain of Gennesaret, which, as we have seen, Josephus called "the ambition of nature." In a cave in the hills of Galilee overlooking this plain was found the skull of the Galilee man, dating back perhaps to 100,000 years ago. Capernaum was a border station on the great highway that led from Syria and Transjordan to Palestine. Consequently, it had a toll post, which is mentioned in the Gospels. Capernaum became famous, because it was there that Jesus took up his abode after leaving Nazareth. The home of Peter became "the house of Jesus." Immediately after his arrival at Capernaum, "straightway on the sabbath day he entered into the synagogue, and taught" (Mark 1:21). The partly restored ruins of a magnificent successor to this synagogue, built several centuries later, can be seen at Capernaum today (Fig. 32). Constructed in basilica fashion, it was oriented toward Jerusalem. The walls were decorated with lovely friezes depicting palms, vines and grapes, acanthus leaves, pomegranates, garlands, and mythological forms. There were also the seven-branched candlestick and the six-pointed star. On the walls of the contemporary synagogue at Chorazin (Fig. 33), a few miles above Capernaum, were sculptured pagan symbols, which, like those at Capernaum, had lost religious significance for the Jews. Among them were a Medusa head and a centaur struggling with a lion. Other friezes included carvings of a man, with a staff in his raised right hand and a bunch of grapes in his lowered left hand, and representations of birds and animals and plants of various kinds.

The people of Chorazin and Capernaum, as well as Bethsaida, "wherein most of his mighty works were done," were upbraided by Jesus "because they repented not" (Matt. 11:20–24). An Aramaic inscription scratched on a limestone pillar at Capernaum reads: "HLPW, the son of Zebidah, the son of Johanan, made this column. May blessing be his." Those names correspond roughly to the New Testament Alphaeus, Zebedee, and John, mentioned, by an interesting coincidence, in the list of Jesus' disciples and their families (Mark 3:17, 18). In the synagogue of Chorazin there was discovered a stone chair of the type reserved for the most distinguished of the elders of the synagogue. Incised on it was an Aramaic inscription which read: "Remembered be for good Judan bar Ishmael, who made this *stoa* and its footstool. As his reward, may he have a share with the righteous." The discovery of this *kathedra* at Chorazin illuminates the passage in Matt. 23:2 which speaks of "the seat of Moses."

The banks of the Jordan know no more storied site than that of Bethsaida, the "Fisherman's Village." Located not far from Capernaum, it stood perhaps on the east side of the Jordan, near the point where it enters the Lake of Galilee. Its pattern conformed to that of proud Paneas, having had indeed the same architect. We read in Josephus: "When Philip . . . had built Paneas . . . at the fountains of Jordan, he named it Cesarea. He also advanced the village Bethsaida, situated at the lake of Gennesareth, unto the dignity of a city, both by the number of inhabitants it contained, and its other grandeur, and called it by the name of Julias, the same name with Caesar's [Augustus] daughter" (*The Jewish Antiquities*, XVIII: ii. 1). It was to Bethsaida that Jesus withdrew upon hearing of the beheading of John the Baptist by Herod Antipas in accordance with the supplication of Salome (Matt. 14: 6–12; Mark 6: 22–29). Near Bethsaida is a desert place (Mark 6:31, 32; Matt. 14:13), which is the supposed scene of the miracle of feeding the five thousand (Luke 9: 10–17).

In recent years were discovered the ruins of a fine Byzantine basilica, commemorating the feeding of the five thousand. It is located

FIG. 32. The partly restored ruins of the early synagogue at Capernaum, which probably replaced the one in which Jesus preached.

FIG. 33. The synagogue at Chorazin, with this vintage scene on one of its stones, was built several centuries after the time of Jesus.

on the western shore of the Lake of Galilee, just below 'Ain Tabgha, between Capernaum and Tiberias. The basilica is now known as the Church of the Multiplication of the Loaves and Fishes. Built into the altar was a large, rough, limestone boulder, which apparently was thought to have been the rock upon which Jesus placed the five loaves and two fishes. Between the altar and the apse is a mosaic, showing a basket containing four small, round wafers of bread, each marked with a cross. The fifth wafer is not visible. On each side of the basket is a fish. The mosaic floors of the north and south transepts are adorned with pictorial representations of such beauty that they are hardly equaled by any other Palestinian Church mosaics, except perhaps some of those from Byzantine Beisan. Oleander bushes, rushes, lotus and papyrus plants are woven in against a light background. In between them are to be seen ducks, geese, storks, peacocks, herons, and flamingos, which seem to be nibbling blossoms or attacking snakes. Smaller birds are depicted balancing themselves on branches of trees or preening their feathers. Particularly attractive are a pair of birds, placed in a large lotus blossom, caressing each other with their beaks. In the midst of all the colorful flora and fauna, pictures of various buildings have been placed, including a Nilometer. This basilica, built about A.D. 400, was repaired later on, after having been damaged by an earthquake. It was destroyed early in the seventh century A.D. by either the Persians or the Arabs.

6

The preaching of Jesus, like the lessons taught in the synagogues of the time, was far removed from the religions that had once held sway along the shores of the Lake of Galilee and the banks of the River Jordan. The nature of one of these early forms of religion is suggested by the name of an ancient site situated close to the Jordan River, as it emerges from the south end of the Lake of Galilee once again an independent stream. It is a long, low mound called Khirbet Kerak, which has been identified with the Beth-yerah of yore. Now Beth-yerah means the "Temple of the Moon," testifying to the fact that in early times, near the end of the fourth millennium B.C., and again about the second quarter of the third millennium B.C., the cult of the moon god or goddess was carried on there. This applies also to pre-Israelite Jericho, in which name too is contained clear intimation of devotion to a lunar deity. From moon worship to worship of the idea of one invisible Father of all mankind was a long step forward in the history of human thinking. From the prehistoric Galilee man to Jeremiah and Jesus represents a prodigious degree of development in the human species.

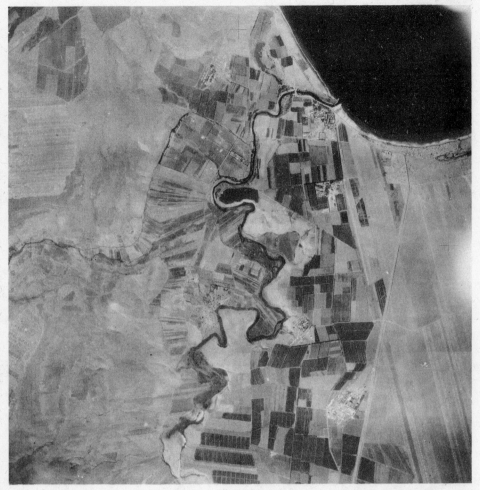

Photo by Royal Air Force, Levant

FIG. 34. The River Jordan leaving the south end of the Lake of Galilee, with the modern Jewish agricultural colony of Dagania at its right and the Arab town of Samakh beyond it at the foot of the lake.

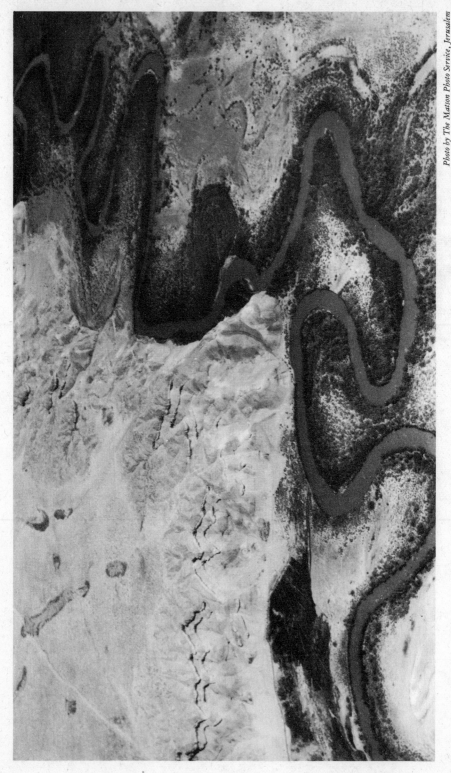

Photo by The Matson Photo Service, Jerusalem

Fig. 35. In wild twists and loops the Jordan winds its way southward through its Jungle or *Zor*, invisible to anyone standing on the *Ghor* level of the valley above it.

III

"A Garden of God"

I

AT THE SOUTH END of the Lake of Galilee, the coast opens out again, marking the beginning of the Jordan Valley, here about 4 miles wide. Pouring out of the lake like a stream from the bottom of a funnel, the Jordan cuts its way through the valley, turning first due west, and then striking south along the base of the hills (Fig. 34). From here on the Jordan passes through no more lakes until it reaches the Dead Sea, in which it loses itself completely. From that body of water there is no outlet. The valley through which the river flows between the Lake of Galilee and the Dead Sea is about 65 miles long, and from 3 to 14 miles wide. The river itself, however, twists and turns in quarter and half and three-quarter loops (Fig. 35) for a total length of some 200 miles.

The Jordan Valley falls 590 feet, or an average of about 9 feet a mile, in the direct distance between the bodies of sweet and salt water. It can be imagined therefore that in spite of its intestinelike configuration within the frame of the valley, the current of the Jordan is a swift one. Whirlpools, rapids (Fig. 36), and small cascades appear frequently along its length. Today a sluice gate regulates the flow of water from the lake into the river, in connection with the Rutenberg hydroelectric plant near the junction of the Yarmuk and Jordan Rivers. There a dam has been built, creating a reservoir, into which the waters of both rivers are led. From this reservoir the water plunges down through chutes nearly 90 feet high to create electrical power sufficient to serve the needs of a large part of Palestine (Fig. 37). With no diminution of their quantity, the waters of both rivers reach the main bed of the Jordan through a new channel (Fig. 38).

The Jordan from the Lake of Galilee southward is about 90 to 100 feet broad, and from about 3 to 10 feet deep. Those figures vary naturally in the springtime, when the river is in flood, and the waters rise to cover a much wider bed. By the time the river has reached the point where the Yarmuk flows into it, it has lost its Galilean clearness, and become muddy as well as turbulent. From then on it has a treacherous, zigzag current, which tears from one side to the other, bent apparently upon undercutting and dumping into the Dead Sea as much of its banks as it possibly can. Let those familiar from story and song with the River Jordan, who imagine it to be a mighty stream as broad and long as the Mississippi or the Ohio, remember that it is rather to be compared to one of the smaller tributaries of these two majestic rivers.

History has magnified the Jordan in the thinking of reverent or merely interested millions out of all proportion to its actual size. To be sure, its basic importance cannot be magnified, because its role in history has been great beyond all rational measurement. Indeed, all of Palestine is no larger than New Hampshire or Vermont. But Palestine bears no comparison with anything else. It combines everything from the temperate to the tropical, from high hills to the lowest valley in the world, from the snows of Hermon which feed the Jordan to the Dead Sea in which the river is drowned. Palestine has always seemed to distill extremes. The developing appreciation of God as we know him today has been its most fruitful achievement. It is in connection with the revelation of the divine that the importance of the Jordan becomes paramount, exceeding that of any other river in the world.

2

The present line of the Jordan is a zigzag ditch carved crazily through the center of its long valley. Its ever-present concern seems to be to deepen the geological fault whose initial appearance made its formation inevitable. The fickle stream, frequently bored with its narrow bed, changes its position as often as possible. There are numerous abandoned bends, through which for the nonce it no longer deigns to run. It leaves them aside as though it were a serpent shedding its skin (Fig. 39). At floodtime in the spring, it bursts its banks to frolic within the confines of its depression, called in Arabic the *Zor*, "thicket," which is from 200 yards to a mile wide. Unlike the Nile, however, the annual flood leaves no blessing in its wake. It carries away at least as much earth as it leaves behind it, and it befouls the land with debris of all kinds.

The narrow flood plain of the *Zor*, through which the Jordan knifes its way, is tropical in character, and, for the most part, lush green in color. Its vegetation is rank, and thorn and thistle grow shoulder high. It is covered with dense and at times almost impenetrable thickets of oleander, cane, tangled bushes, vines, willows, poplars, and twisted tamarisks. From the air it looms like a slimy green snake, standing out all the more startlingly because of the desert white and dirty gray of its surroundings. In Biblical times it was known as the *Ge'on hay-Yarden*, that is, the "Jungle of the Jordan." (It is usually translated as the "Pride of the Jordan.") And a very good name it was. Lions once had their lairs there, and it is still haunted by jackals and wolves. "Behold he shall come up like a lion from the Jungle of the Jordan against the strong habitation" (Jer. 49:19). We can now understand Jer. 12:5: "And though in a land of peace thou art secure, yet how wilt thou do in the Jungle of the Jordan?" (Fig. 40).

At one place in the *Zor*, or Jungle, the Jordan makes a three-quarter bend around a fertile section of flat land, bounded on the east by rising hills (Fig. 41). It is a little, hidden paradise, with several springs of its own. Although empty of inhabitants today, in its center stands an ancient mound. The pottery found on its surface indicates that it was occupied in the days of the kings of Israel. Whence came and whither have gone the settlers who tilled the soil in this lonely place cut off from all except casual contact with the outside world? Was it pressure of population or a particular community of interests that made them move to this secluded corner? Today it is called *el-Meqbereh*, the "Burial Place," and is visited infrequently by Arabs to bury their dead.

Fig. 36. The swirling, twisting Jordan makes islands, forms new channels, and abandons old ones.

Photo by Keren Hayesod, Jerusalem

FIG. 37. Artificial lake of Palestine Electric Corporation formed by diversion of Yarmuk (upper right) and Jordan rivers into it. The waters flow through a canal to the powerhouse. They escape finally through an artificial channel (lower left) into the Jordan.

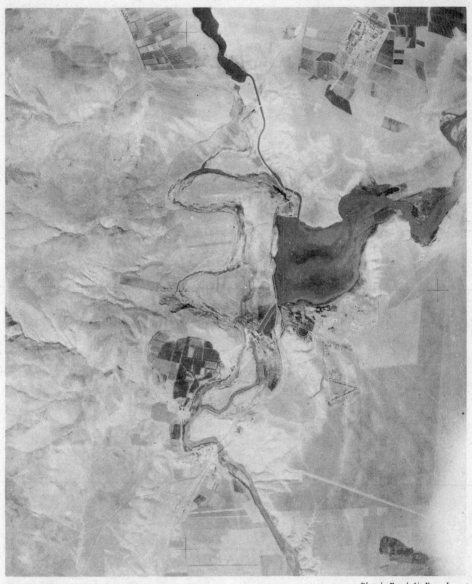

FIG. 38. Palestine Electric Corporation lake formed by diversion of Jordan and Yarmuk rivers into it. After being led down an artificial 90-foot drop to create electrical power, the waters are turned back into the Jordan river bed to continue their normal flow southward. The waters of the Jordan held back by sluice gates are led through a canal to the lake, which is fed also by the waters of the Yarmuk (right).

Photo by The Matson Photo Service, Jerusalem

FIG. 39. "The present line of the Jordan is a zigzag ditch carved crazily through the center of its long valley."

Photo by Keren Hayesod, Jerusalem

FIG. 40. The Jungle of the Jordan. Though the Jordan here is swift, it meanders like a lazy tidewater stream through the narrow flood plain of the Jungle of the Jordan. Eroded white marl hills lead down to it as much as 150 feet from each side of the upper, broader terrace of the Jordan Valley.

68

Photo by The Matson Photo Service, Jerusalem

FIG. 41. A part of the cultivable section of the *Zor*, "thicket," of the Jordan, with the main part of the valley proper, the *Ghor*, "rift," rising about 150 feet above it.

FIG. 42. The Jordan River near Allenby Bridge, showing the vegetation in the *Zor* along its banks, and the whitish marl *qattarah* hills which rise between the *Zor*, and the upper, *Ghor* level of the Jordan Valley.

3

When most people talk about the Jordan Valley, they are really thinking of its upper level, now known as the *Ghor*, "depression," and not of its lower one, the *Zor*, "thicket" (Fig. 42). There is as much as 150 feet difference in height between them. Separating them, and marking the transition from the one to the other, are wildly torn grayish-marl hills, called *qattarahs*, on which practically nothing grows. One may say that there are three terraces, with two steep hill-sides between them, leading to the Jordan, whether approaching it from Palestine to the west or from Transjordan to the east. First comes the broken plateau or hill country of Palestine and Trans-jordan, then the steep, jagged descent to the Jordan Valley, from which, in turn, desert-dead hills lead down to the Jungle of the Jor-dan or the *Zor*. In it, the river weaves its erratic way (see frontispiece). I have seen fighter planes skimming along at terrific speed low over the *Zor*, hidden from sight below the wild hills that border its banks, and invisible to anyone standing in the valley itself above it.

The name most commonly employed in the Bible to describe the main part of the Jordan Valley is *Kikkar hay-Yarden*, as distinguished from the narrower and lower part, called, as we have seen, *Ge'on hay-Yarden*. The existence of these two distinctive sections of the Jordan Valley is described in the *Official Report of the United States Expedition to Explore the Dead Sea and the Jordan River*, as follows: "There are evidently two terraces to the Jordan, and through the lowest one the river runs its serpentine course. From the stream above the immediate banks, there is, on each side, a singular terrace of low hills, like trun-cated cones, which is the bluff terminus of an extended table land." Headed by Lieutenant Commander W. F. Lynch, this expedition explored the Jordan and the Dead Sea in the year 1848, using small boats specially constructed for the purpose. Now, nearly a century later, an expedition supported in part by The Smithsonian Insti-tution of the United States National Museum, in co-operation with the American School of Oriental Research in Jerusalem, has explored archaeologically, for the first time in history, the entire east side of the Jordan Valley. The "extended table land" about which Lieutenant Commander Lynch wrote, is to be identified with the Biblical *Kikkar hay-Yarden*, which means the "encircled Jordan Valley." The name applies also to separate parts of it. Contained in an incomparably deep hollow, the valley is enclosed for its total length by high hills on either side. Sometimes sections of it are referred to as *'emeq*, that is, the "Deep Valley," or as *biq'ah*, the "Opening Out," or "Fissure," or as *'arabah*, the "Plain."

The Jordan Valley has been much maligned. It has generally been assumed that it has "never been populous," that most of the mounds in it "are probably the remains not of cities but of old brick fields," that towns have "always been few in the Valley," and that it has "deserved the name of Wilderness."[1] Four main reasons have been advanced for this supposed state of affairs: intolerable heat, malignant malaria, wild beasts, and savage men. All these reasons are based upon superficial knowledge of the actual conditions in the valley.

I have spent months riding along its entire east side, and much of its west side, sleeping each night in a different Arab tent. I would make a point of asking my hosts about the so-called terrible weather and living conditions, excluding, of course, the Jungle of the Jordan. Invariably they replied that life in the valley was not considered at all intolerable. With few exceptions, the Arabs stay there all the year round. While many of them suffer from malaria, they are no more afflicted than are the inhabitants of numerous parts of the highlands of Palestine and Transjordan. As for the heat, it is bearable, although at times admittedly burdensome. Many Europeans have lived in recent years in the valley, without any apparent impairment of their health. And we have already seen that its climate has not changed from early prehistoric times. Furthermore, it is not now, and in historical times never has been, overrun by wild animals, although the deeper Jungle of the Jordan has had a large number of them. Its most dangerous beasts have always been two-legged ones. The story of the settlement of men there belies the belief that, with a few exceptions, the presence of savages has kept it a wasteland.

[1] Smith, George Adam, *op. cit.*, pp. 487ff.

Our recent explorations in the Jordan Valley have shown beyond doubt that it was once densely inhabited. Large and small settlements dotted the land. Excellent pottery was produced. Highly intensive agriculture was practiced. Thriving civilizations flourished. On the east side of the Jordan alone we discovered more than seventy ancient sites, many of them founded more than five thousand years ago, and some of them earlier. Let there be no more prattle then of empty wilderness in the Jordan Valley!

It would have been well if previous writers had first looked for information about it in the annals of the Bible. "And Lot lifted up his eyes, and he beheld all the Valley of the Jordan. And lo, all of it was irrigated, . . . and it was like a garden of God" (Gen. 13:10). Now Lot may frequently have been wrong in the eyes of his shrewish wife, who to be sure apparently got her just deserts, but he was certainly right when it came to describing the Jordan Valley. It is true that his description was meant only for its lower part, including the entire Jericho area and the Plains of Moab, but it applies equally well to almost all the rest of the Jordan Valley. It is possible to say now that the Jordan Valley was not only one of the first settled sections of the country, but that it was also one of the richest parts of all ancient Palestine and Transjordan. It remains today potentially what it was then indubitably, a garden of God.

4

It was through the Jordan Valley, in all probability, that Abram, later to become known as Abraham, pursued and caught up with the kidnapers of Lot, who had fled with much booty of captives and goods when Sodom fell. The chase was fast and far. Not until he and his followers got to Dan, by one of the sources of the Jordan, could battle be joined with the enemy. "And they [Chedorlaomer and his confederates] took all the goods of Sodom and Gomorrah, and all their victuals, and went their way. And they took Lot, . . . who dwelt in Sodom, and his goods, and departed. Then there came one that had escaped, and told Abram the Hebrew, who dwelt by the oaks of Mamre. . . . And when Abram heard that his brother was taken captive, he led forth his trained men, born in his house, three hundred and eighteen, and pursued as far as Dan. And he divided himself against them by night, he and his servants, and smote them and pursued them unto Hobah, which is on the left hand of Damascus. And he brought back his brother Lot, and his goods, and the women also, and the people" (Gen. 14:11–16).

The raiders, striking traditionally as far from home as possible, had suffered a painful surprise. They had been hit hard before they had had opportunity to disperse and dispose of their gain. The forceful sheikh, Abram, had lost little time in his tent under the trees near Hebron after news of the disaster had reached him. Tribal loyalty left him little choice. Harm done to any of his group was his own hurt. Gathering together all his effectives, a swift-moving band of 318 fighting men, he sped to rescue and revenge. I believe the figure of 318 to be exactly correct, although aware of the fact that it had to be repeated from father to son for well over a thousand years before there was any possibility of committing it to paper. To this very day there are old men in the tents of Arabia who can recite the history of their ancestors for forty generations, and if in their recital they stray but a jot from the facts, others within hearing will immediately correct them, or supply forgotten details.

If, as we have assumed, Abram's march led through the Jordan Valley, then his journey was a relatively easy one. Food and water could be found on the way. He who was famous for hospitality would not lack for a hearty welcome wherever he turned. Had he been a complete stranger, however, he would have been received no less warmly. Time and again I have halted my horse near an Arab tent in the Jordan Valley, to have its occupants run out, grasp the reins, and beg me to dismount and stay with them (Fig. 43). Even before the guests entered the shade of their "house of hair," a happy bustle would begin, to prepare for them. Mattresses would be spread out, rugs laid, camel saddles moved into position to rest on while reclining, the coals of the fire stirred to prepare the warming drink. Had not Abraham himself acted thus to unknown wayfarers, "as he sat in the tent door in the heat of the day"? "And he lifted up his eyes

FIG. 43. Abdul Hamid ibn Emir Hamzeh el-Ya'qub, in front of his father's guest tent in camp near Jisr Sheikh Hussein, on the east side of the Jordan.

Fig. 44. 'Ain Ifdan, one of the few springs in the Wadi Arabah.

and looked, and, lo, three men stood over against him: and when he saw them, he ran to meet them from the tent door, and bowed himself to the earth, and said, . . . Let now a little water be fetched, and wash your feet, and rest yourselves under the tree: and I will fetch a morsel of bread, and strengthen ye your heart; after that ye shall pass on. . . . And they said, So be it. . . . And Abraham hastened into the tent unto Sarah, and said, Make ready quickly three measures of fine meal, knead it, and make cakes. And Abraham ran unto the herd, and fetched a calf tender and good, and gave it unto the servant; and he hasted to dress it . . . and set it before them; and he stood by them under the tree, and they did eat" (Gen. 18:1–8).

5

It may well have been, however, that Abraham and his company of warriors tarried hardly at all on their way after the enemy. They could easily have filled their saddlebags with provender sufficient for their slender needs for several days. I journeyed once with an Arab camel train for thirteen successive days in the wild desert of the Wadi Arabah, which is largely empty, except at infrequent intervals, even of water (Fig. 44). My companions had for food a mean sack of flour and the nightly milk of a camel. It is surprising what distances can be traversed if beasts and riders are pushed. On another occasion, some of us left Aqabah, the seaport of the Wadi Arabah, which is the southern extension of the Jordan fault. We were heading northward for the Dead Sea, some 110 miles away. By the time we had loaded our camels, darkness had snuffed out the day, bringing quick blackness. We mounted and rode northward by the light of a full moon, shining in cloudless, dry skies. The camels stepped out protestingly. But then camels are the most confirmed pessimists and grumblers I have yet met. No matter what you do with them, they grumble. If you shift your weight in the saddle, they grumble. If you make them kneel, they grumble. If you tap them on their long necks with the driving cane to quicken their pace, they grumble. They believe in grumbling first, last, and always.

We were five men and five camels all told on that trip. With us

rode Sheikh Audeh ibn Jad, the head of the Injadat Arabs who live
on the Transjordan side of the Wadi Arabah (Fig. 45). The Injadat
Arabs are thought by many to be the descendants of the ancient
Gadites, one of the two and a half tribes (Reuben, Gad, and half the
tribe of Manasseh) that settled on the east side of the Jordan.
Whether or not Audeh ibn Jad is actually a lineal descendant of some
sheikh of the tribe of Gad is a moot question. But I can testify that
he is a perfect gentleman, a born leader, and a splendid companion,
full of wit and wisdom. Abraham may well have looked like him.

   The night grew, and peace settled over us. We watched the evening
stars peep over the hills of Edom, and then, with mounting boldness,
climb high into the heavens. The moon lighted our way with inde-
fatigable brilliance. Sometimes we rode five abreast, and frequently
in single file. And I thought of the ancient Israelites, who trekked
north along the path we were following to Punon, which the Bible
tells us they reached in the course of their wanderings from Sinai to
the Promised Land (Num. 33:43). The hours lengthened, and the
cold penetrated our tightly hugged cloaks. These were Arab *abayas* of
hand-woven woollen cloth, little different, in all probability, from the
kind Abraham had once used. After five hours in the saddle, we decided to call a brief halt. The camels were made to kneel, a bright
fire of dry brush was started up, and some hot soup was prepared
that tasted like nectar. The camels were given a feed of barley, which
they grumblingly accepted. We slept awhile. Soon we mounted
again, being shaken to complete wakefulness as the camels lurched
drunkenly to standing position and then swayed forward with long-
paced steadiness. Dawn broke, the sun rose, first to warm and then
to roast us. All day long we rode. When the day was done, half the
trip was over. We could have made the rest of the distance to the
Dead Sea in another such push if we had been so minded.

   In such wise, Abraham and his men may have dashed by forced
marches from Hebron to the Dead Sea, and from the Dead Sea along
the Jordan Valley, to waylay and discomfit the raiders overtaken at
Dan at its northern end. Records do not reveal whether or not he
tarried along the way. Suffice it to say that in his time, near the be-

FIG. 45. Sheikh Audeh ibn Jad, of the Injadat Arabs, and Sheikh Suleiman, of the Saidiyin.
The name of Jad suggests a possible connection with the ancient tribe of Gad.

ginning of the second millennium B.C., there were numerous settlements of imposing size along this road through the valley, many of them of a highly developed nature. Some people, however, preferred living in tents part of the year, just as many Arabs do today. Others slept only under tent roofs all the year round, moving their camping spot every month or two when the ground had become soiled.

6

In the springtime of Israel, the sanctuary of the Lord was in the Tent of Testimony. Later it was to be displaced by the Phoenician Temple of Solomon. The simplicity of the tent is sweet to the heart of the unspoiled Semite, and the life and social organization that go with it are preferred to much treasure. Kings and palaces and permanent stone houses are repugnant to him. With crystal clairvoyance the Prophet Samuel portrayed the evil possibilities of earthly kings when presenting his objections to the appointment of one of them over the people of Israel, who insisted upon being like other nations. "This will be the manner of the king that shall reign over you," he said. "He will take your sons, and appoint them unto him, for his chariots, and to be his horsemen. . . . And he will set some to plow his ground, and to reap his harvest, and to make his instruments of war. . . . And he will take your daughters . . . and . . . your fields, and your vineyards, and your olive groves. . . . And ye shall cry out in that day because of your king" (I Sam. 8:11–18). More extreme even than he in recalling the Israelites to their Spartan beginnings were the Rechabites. They were closely related in habit and thought to the early prophets of Israel, who initiated the tendency to idealize the early days in the desert.

The Rechabites followed the precept of their founder: "Jonadab the son of Rechab, our founder, commanded us saying, Ye shall drink no wine, . . . nor sow seed, nor plant vineyards, nor have any. But all your days ye shall dwell in tents: that ye may live many days in the land wherein ye sojourn" (Jer. 35:6, 7). It is no accident that their doctrines were in harmony with the teachings and activities of Elijah and Elisha, in whose lives the Jordan figured so prominently.

Nor is it strange that the later Essenes, to whom John the Baptist may have been indebted, had much in common with them. Philo says of the Essenes: "Among all men, they alone are without money and without possessions, but are nevertheless the richest of all, because to have few wants and to live frugally they regard as riches. Among them is no maker of any weapons of war, . . . nor do they follow any occupation that leads to injustice and covetousness."[1] Many of these humble and modest Essenes, whose influence upon earliest Christianity was large, were at home in the Jordan Valley, particularly in the neighborhood of Jericho.

7

Exuberantly rich earth and an abundance of water are the immediate and most apparent reasons for the former prosperity of the Jordan Valley. The valley is a great catchment basin for water, not only from the snows of Hermon and the seasonal rains, but also from the tributaries reaching it from the west and east, which tap thousands of square miles. It is amazing to see how the thirsty valley opens up wide to receive these waters. It fairly unfolds to be made fruitful by them. For a distance of some 13 miles, starting from the Lake of Galilee, it is little more and sometimes less than 4 miles wide. Where the Nahr (River) Jalud descends through the plain of Beisan to the Jordan River, the valley throws its arms about it, as if to say, "Welcome, my beloved." Here the valley is from 6 to 7 miles across. Soon, however, the starved hills of Samaria press in severely to break the embrace. They practically trample upon the floor of the valley, which, perforce, pulls itself together, and narrows down to slender proportions. Farther south, the Wadi Far'ah cleaves its way through the austere hills, and forces them to retreat. Relieved of their presence, the Jordan Valley elbows its way into a space 8 miles across. It continues then to expand as it grows longer, so that by the time it reaches the Jericho area it has achieved its maximum width of 14 miles.

[1] *Quod Omnis Probus Liber Sit*, Article 12.

FIG. 46. The Arnon river and gorge (Wadi Mojib) near its outlet into the Dead Sea.

IV

The Highlands of Transjordan

I

THE STREAMS on the east side of the Jordan are larger, more numerous, and more valuable than those on the west side. They stretch out their branches eastward to the line between the Desert and the Sown. Gathering strength from numerous sources, they slash their way deeply across the country, severing it into distinctive segments. Among the most important of these streams emptying into the Jordan from the east are the Yarmuk in the north, the Zerqa in the center, and the Hesban in the south. Below them are the Mojib and the Hesa, which empty into the Dead Sea. Most of them are known by name in the Bible, and figure frequently in its accounts. The Zerqa is the Biblical Jabbok, the Mojib is the Biblical Arnon, and the Hesa is the Biblical Zered. All of them are smaller than the Jordan. The beds in which they flow all the year round are at the bottom of mighty canyons, with sides so steep that only in recent years have modern roads been blasted across them. These were preceded by Trajan's Roman Road, which ran from Syria to the Red Sea, and by the still earlier "Highway of the King." "And Moses sent messengers from Qadesh [Kadesh] unto the king of Edom [saying], . . . Let us pass, I pray thee, through thy land. . . . We will go along the king's highway, turning neither to the right nor to the left, until we have passed thy border. And Edom said unto him, Thou shalt not pass through me, lest I come out with the sword against thee. . . . Wherefore Israel turned away from him" (Num. 20:14–21).

2

The Zered marked the northern limit of ancient Edom. Esau wandered there, sore in spirit, after having been cheated out of his birthright and the blessing of the first-born by his brother Jacob. The

Israelites of the Exodus had to go east around Edom, whose numerous fortifications and strong cities barred their way directly through it. At a much later time, events took place in Edom which were to have their repercussions upon happenings in the Jordan Valley and elsewhere. Some of the Edomites infiltrated into southern Palestine, where, in Hellenistic-Roman times, they became known as Idumaeans. They had in part been pushed out of Edom by the Nabataeans, who had entered Edom and Moab in strength from Arabia. Herod Antipas and Herod Philip, sons of the Idumaean Herod the Great, had, respectively, built Tiberias, on the Lake of Galilee, and Caesarea Philippi, by one of the sources of the Jordan. Herod the Great himself had rebuilt Jericho and other places in the Jordan Valley in Greco-Roman style. It was the governor of Damascus, ruling in the name of the Nabataean king, Aretas IV (9 B.C.–A.D. 40), who attempted to imprison Paul when he came out of the desert. Paul himself wrote of his escape: "In Damascus the governor under Aretas the king guarded the city of the Damascenes in order to take me: and through a window was I let down in a basket by the wall, and escaped his hands" (II Cor. 11:32, 33).

3

The River Arnon (Fig. 46) was the northern boundary of the kingdom of Moab at the time of the advent of the Israelites. The rest of Moab north of it had been seized by Sihon, king of the Amorites. He dwelt at Heshbon (modern Ḥesbân), by the stream of that name, which empties into the Jordan just above its outlet into the Dead Sea. The Israelites burst through his territory on their way to the Jordan, after Edom and Moab, according to one of the Biblical accounts, had refused them transit through their lands. As a result of these refusals, they "went around the land of Edom, and the land of Moab, and . . . encamped on the other side of the Arnon; but they came not within the border of Moab, for the Arnon was the border of Moab" (Judg. 11:18).

From Moab came Ruth, who was to be redeemed from widowhood by marriage with Boaz of Bethlehem, her first husband's kinsman. Tradition has made her, this non-Israelitess, the ancestress of David, in whose house was vested Messianic hope. And the genealogy of Jesus is described as going back to David. Like Edom, Moab was a lovely land. It was full of fine cities, and blessed with fat acres and great flocks of sheep and goats. "Now Mesha king of Moab was a sheep-master; and he rendered unto the king of Israel the wool of a hundred thousand lambs, and of a hundred thousand rams" (II Kings 3:4). To this day Moab is famous for its flocks, which thrive on rich pasturage. Its strongly built stone cities—and I have examined scores of them—were surrounded by high walls entered through elaborate gates. No wonder they appeared to the nomads as "fortified up to heaven" and inhabited by giants.

Such was the Moabite city of Qir-hareseth, now known as Kerak. It was built on top of an impregnable hill, through which was pierced an almost vertical tunnel, tapping a secure water supply. The massive castle, perched like a powerful eagle on a commanding crag, is Crusader in origin, Moslem in repair, and modern in decay (Figs. 47, 48). In the lime between the great blocks of its crippled wings I have found fragments of Nabataean pottery, contemporary with the time of Christ. The present ruins evidently replaced a Nabataean stronghold, which had probably been built on the wreckage of the Moabite fortress. Nought is left there of the Moabite period except the figure of a brooding lion on a building stone, and brilliantly ornamented potsherds testifying to highly skilled workmanship. An ancient road led from Kerak to the Dead Sea and to the Jordan. Flying over it, I have been amazed at the modernity of its appearance.

4

From the Mount of Olives in Jerusalem the highlands of Moab can be seen frowning over the Dead Sea basin and the southern part of the Jordan fault. They are about 2,500 feet above sea level, and about 3,800 feet above the surface of the Dead Sea. A purple haze, tinctured with red and gray, softens the abrupt drop from the bountiful plateau to the baneful sea. The Israelites approaching the Land of Promise descended from the high hills of Moab to the fields of Moab

Photo by Govt. of Palestine, Dept. of Antiquities

FIG. 47. Crusader castle of Kerak, looking at west side. It occupies the site of the Biblical Qir-hareseth.

Photo by Govt. of Palestine, Dept. of Antiquities

Fig. 48. Passageway inside Crusader castle of Kerak.

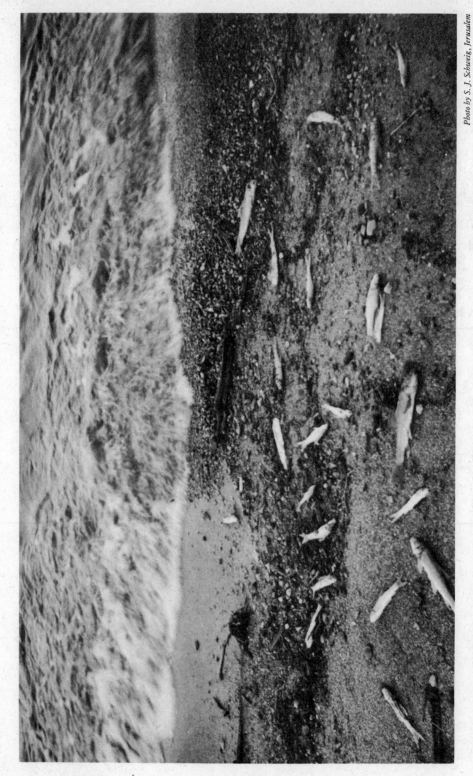

Photo by S. J. Schweig, Jerusalem

FIG. 49. Fish from the Arnon River (Wadi Mojib), killed by the dense salt waters of the Dead Sea and washed ashore.

FIG. 50. The Roman theater at Amman, Transjordan, anciently known as Philadelphia, one of the cities of the Decapolis.

far below, at the northeast end of the sea. From the vantage point of the eastern hills of Jerusalem the practiced glance may discern where the western edge of the Moabite plateau is cleft by the Arnon as it cuts a deep canyon through it.

I have never yet looked east toward the hills of Moab without being seized by a sense of excitement. I have never yet started climbing steeply toward their tops without wondering what new mystery would reveal itself to me. For these lands, east as well as west of the Jordan, are haunted by the shades of history and throb with the pulse of the past. These are more than conglomerations of rock and soil, with springs and plants, animals and people. These are the haunts of the children of God, and his Spirit is imprinted in the very atmosphere. I have stood on the shores of the Red Sea and heard the accents of Jehovah in Sinai. I have wandered in the wastes of the desert and heard the weeping of Hagar. I have sat in the tents of Ishmael and found myself peering into the faces of prophets. I have paced along the banks of the Jordan and watched the people of Israel crossing over to the Land of Promise.

5

One morning four of us started down from the edge of the plateau of Moab in search of an ancient site, reputed to exist somewhere near the base of the jagged slope far below. The night before, over the coffeepot kept hot in smoldering embers, the crowded tent rang with the praises of the Ruin of Riyashi. Tongues and imaginations were loosened, and born raconteurs embroidered what turned out to be a shred of fact with a web of fancy. Was indeed the story made of whole cloth? But then our map did vaguely mark the position of such a place, and several shepherds, independently questioned, had agreed that it actually existed. None of them, however, could describe its location with any more exactness than might be imparted with a wave of the hand, and with the confident reassurance, that *inshallah*,"by the grace of Allah," we would unquestionably find it. Could anyone guide us? A poor fellow was finally presented, who for a fair penny professed to be able to lead the way. So off we went,

Reginald Head, then of the Transjordan Department of Antiquities, Ali Abu Ghosh, my faithful companion, who always dragged his heavy rifle with him, the guide, and myself.

The descent was fast and furious. Frequently we kept ourselves upright by digging our heels in deeply and leaning backward as we went downward. At first there had been several terraces or benches of land interposed between hillsides, but after a while there was nothing but a succession of steep slopes. Soon it became apparent that the guide had joined us for the gift he expected to receive, and not for the information he was able to impart. I heard Ali Abu Ghosh muttering explosive imprecations. "May sand cover up his eyes," was the mildest of them, as he looked balefully at the miscreant who was misleading us.

Finally we did manage to find the Ruin of Riyashi, more than three thousand feet below our starting point. It had become obvious that whatever might be found could not be of much importance, because these jagged hillsides could never have supported much of a population. It turned out to be a small Byzantine monastery, nesting on the flat top of an outspur surrounded on three sides by the waters of the Arnon. In this quiet retreat, cut off from the turbulence of the outside world, monks sought quiet communion with God. The remains of a few terraced fields on the north side of the stream showed how they had tried to eke out a meager existence. They probably also had a few goats. Men can learn to live on very little. A few miles farther on, the Arnon, rushing through an echoing canyon with walls so steep that the sun penetrates into it only part of the day, flows into the Dead Sea (Fig. 49). The last part of its course is marked by rapids and waterfalls. Unlike the Jordan, it is almost as clear at its outlet as at its beginning.

It took several hours to finish planning and photographing the site. The sun, veering to the west on this hot summer day, was hitting us hard as we began to climb up the east side of the caldron in which we were caught. The brackish water with which we had filled our canteens was soon finished. The heat grew more intense, and our exhaustion mounted apace. After a while it became possible to make progress only by resting for fifteen minutes after walking ten. The Arab guide collapsed. We propped him up on a ledge and left him. Now we were halfway up the hill, continuing by sheer will power at a crawling pace. No words were wasted. Our lips swelled and cracked. I threw away everything I was carrying except my notebook and camera. At about five o'clock Ali collapsed. I shall not soon forget how he looked, as, lying on the ground, he gasped to me: "*Iza kan ma tejibsh li moya, ana bamut*" (If you don't bring me some water, I shall die). I loosened his collar, and wiped his lips clean of dried foam. Head and I struggled on. Finally I was done in and simply could not continue. Suddenly it just didn't matter any more. The earth seemed to rise to meet me, and I hugged it. I felt like a child running into its mother's arms when hurt or frightened. Head, good old Head, carried on until, after what seemed to be ages later, he stumbled on a small spring and dropped exhausted. There several Arabs found him, and then came for us. At three in the morning we reached the top of the plateau, having left it at seven the previous morning. Later we heard that our guide had been rescued too.

It becomes understandable, therefore, that the Jordan rift and its continuation, the Wadi Arabah, became a barrier and a boundary between the high countries east and west of it. Like it, to a smaller but no less definite degree, were the great canyons of the Zered, Arnon, Jabbok, and Yarmuk streams, which split the Other Side of the Jordan into geographically self-contained wholes.

The cities of the Jordan Valley, such as Jericho, Beth-shan, and Jabesh-gilead, were, to be sure, not completely cut off from their highland sisters. Part of their importance lay in their location astride the few available roads that lead across the valley from one plateau to the other. The fact remains, however, that most of the inhabitants of the valley never stirred out of it. Neither did their neighbors from the heights above have much occasion to see, or interest in knowing the Jordan Valley, let alone the Jungle of the Jordan, whose terrors had probably been magnified in their hearing.

Little wonder then that Moses was concerned over the request of Reuben, Gad, and half of Manasseh to remain behind and settle in the good lands of pine-clad Gilead, north of Moab, while the rest of the tribes moved westward across the Jordan into the Promised Land. What effect would the separation caused by the valley have upon the continued unity of the Federation? "Bring us not over the Jordan," these would-be secessionists had said to him (Num. 32:5). And he had sharply replied: "Shall your brethren go to war, and shall ye sit here? And wherefore do ye discourage the heart of the children of Israel from going over into the land which the Lord hath given to them?" (vs. 6, 7). They replied reassuringly, however: "Let us build sheepfolds here for our flocks, and cities for our children. We ourselves will be ready to go armed before the children of Israel, until we have brought them to their place. . . . We will not return unto our houses until . . . [they] have inherited every man his inheritance. For we will not inherit with them on the other side of the Jordan; because our inheritance is fallen to us on this side of the Jordan eastward" (vs. 16–19). So it was done, but, just as Moses had foreseen, the connection between the parts of Israel separated by the Jordan Valley became fragile.

6

One of the main streams flowing through the highlands of Transjordan is the River Jabbok (Wadi Zerqa), rising at a spring in Amman, the capital of Transjordan. Rabbath Ammon was the city's full name of old, when it was capital of the kingdom of Ammon. Mute witness of spent glory are the ruins of a Roman theater, built when the town's name was changed for a brief period to Philadelphia, City of Brotherly Love (Fig. 50). The Jabbok flows north for some miles, then turns and pursues a constant course westward through a descending valley narrowing into an ever deeper canyon. Finally its high walls drop away suddenly to a rich plain, which merges with the Jordan Valley. In it are ancient cities, most of whose former names have been completely forgotten. One of them, Succoth, is mentioned in the Bible.

Nahash, king of Ammon, pressed his power as far west as the Jordan Valley. There he laid siege to Jabesh-gilead on its east side.

The inhabitants of the city sought to make terms with him. He agreed, setting, however, a savage stipulation: "And Nahash the Ammonite said unto them, On this condition will I make . . . [a covenant] with you, namely, that all your right eyes be put out. Thus will I lay it for a reproach upon all Israel. And the elders said unto him, Give us seven days' respite, that we may send messengers unto all the borders of Israel; and then, if there be none to save us, we will come out to thee" (I Sam. 11:2, 3). Nahash agreed, being convinced apparently that help would not be forthcoming. What fun it would be to sit and watch his quarry squirm for seven days, before completing his cruelty on them! He had reckoned, however, without his host. Saul, not yet king, but merely a rugged peasant chieftain, who could be seen in the evening "following the oxen out of the field" (v. 5), was roused to wrath when he heard the words of the messengers of Jabesh. Having summoned the yeomen of Israel, he made a forced march by night, descended into the valley, crossed the Jordan, and attacked the unsuspecting Ammonites at dawn, smiting them from early morning "until the heat of the day: and it came to pass, that they that remained were scattered, so that not two of them were left together" (v. 11). The men of Jabesh-gilead long bore this kindness in mind, and the day was to come when they would requite Saul with good for the salvation he had brought them.

In the course of time, Hanun, the son of Nahash, succeeded to his father's throne, and David was well disposed to him. Nahash had perhaps once done a favor for David, or perhaps they had drawn close to each other in their common hostility to Saul. Be that as it may, when Nahash died David sent a deputation to Hanun with a message of condolence. But like father, like son! The churlish youth, accepting ill advice, became convinced that David had sent his servants merely to spy out Rabbath Ammon, and make plans for its capture. "So Hanun took David's servants, and shaved off the one half of their beards, and cut off their garments in the middle, even to their buttocks, and sent them away. When it was told to David, he sent to meet them; for the men were greatly ashamed. And the king said, Tarry at Jericho until your beards be grown, and then return"

(II Sam. 10:4, 5). This was an insult that could not be lightly endured. The Ammonites and their Syrian allies were engaged in battle
and defeated. Not satisfied to let well enough alone, the Syrians
called up new forces, and re-formed their ranks for attack. This time,
David, taking personal command, "gathered all Israel together, and
passed over the Jordan" (v. 17) and inflicted such punishment upon
them, that "the Syrians feared to help the Bene-Ammon any more"
(v. 19). Rabbath Ammon was captured and looted. Ammon, Moab,
and Edom were then successively subjected to David's dominion.

The Jordan and the Jabbok were to figure frequently in David's
life. Ishbaal or Ishbosheth, the sole surviving son of Saul, was set up,
after his father's death, on a shaky throne in Mahanaim, on the north
bank of the Jabbok. His life would have been forfeit to David, the
friend of his brother Jonathan, had he not fled eastward beyond the
Jordan. David, contending for the throne of Saul, had himself
crowned king at Hebron, and after Ishbaal's death ultimately ruled
supreme in Jerusalem. The violence he countenanced, or pretended
piously not to condone, was, however, to pursue him to the end of
his days. He was to be cursed to his face as a "man of blood, and a
base fellow" (ch. 16:7). In the evening of his days, he was to be compelled to forsake the comfort of his palace in Jerusalem, and flee for
his life from his own son Absalom, who in unfilial rebellion had
been, like his father before him, crowned king in turbulent Hebron.

I can see the aged sheikh, David, seated on his donkey, departing
to a fare of flight and danger which had been his daily bread in his
younger days. I can see him and his faithful companions fording the
Jordan, skirts tucked up to avoid the water, and then making brief
camp on the other side. I can see them climbing a steep path leading
up a narrow canyon, with good water at the bottom of it. But wait, is
this not the River Jabbok? And is this not the path leading to that
very Mahanaim, to which Ishbosheth once fled from David, when
David seized the crown in Hebron in usurpation of royal rights?
What thoughts weigh down the weary shoulders of this refugee? No
Nathan is necessary this time to accuse him of having stolen the poor
man's only ewe lamb. The rushing stream, the stabbing thorns, the

frowning hills, shout insistently, "The sin is thine, O David, and vengeance is the Lord's!" What punishment portended? How must he expiate his crimes? Dark forebodings tugged at his heartstrings.

But there at last was Mahanaim, the tents of friends and promise of rest and food. And what a heart-warming welcome they received! "And it came to pass, when David was come to Mahanaim, that Shobi the [friendly] son of Nahash of Rabbah, . . . and Machir, . . . and Barzillai . . . [each contributing from his family's store], brought beds, and basins, and earthen vessels, and wheat and barley and meal, . . . and honey and butter and cheese of the herd, for David, and for the people that were with him, to eat: for they said, The people are weary, and hungry, and thirsty, in the wilderness" (ch. 17: 27–29). How often have I received like food when living with Arabs in their tents! How often have I received from them *dibs*, and *zibdeh*, and *jibneh*, and *dhabiheh*, served with piles of round thin flaps of their lovely unleavened bread: *dibs*, something like honey, usually made of dates; *zibdeh*, butter of sheep or goat or kine; *jibneh*, cheese of various kinds; *dhabiheh*, a sheep or goat, slaughtered at the guest's arrival, cooked and served up on a great platter, filled with rice or *burghul*, roasted grains of wheat. How often has my thirst been quenched with *lebn*, thin sour cream, or *sheninah*, buttermilk! A beaker full of it is heaven to a thirsty man.

David's darkest hour was yet to come. Absalom's army, crossing the Jordan in hot pursuit of the faithful forces of David, was finally allowed to close in battle with them at a place of the latter's choosing, and it was cut to pieces. Absalom had to flee for his life among the rough hills and thick woods of Gilead, in the region known today as the Jebel Ajlun. There towers the ruin of the great medieval castle of Qal'at er-Rabad, a landmark from afar (Figs. 51, 52). The woods of oak and pine are still thick, and to this day one can ride for hours under their shade. My clothes have been torn and face whipped by their branches as I have pushed through them on many occasions. "And Absalom was riding upon his mule, and the mule went under the thick boughs of a great oak, and his hair caught hold of the oak, and he was taken up between heaven and earth. And the mule that

Photo by Nelson Glueck

FIG. 51. Medieval Arabic castle of Qal'at er-Rabad, above Ajlun.

Photo by Govt. of Palestine, Dept. of Antiquities

FIG. 52. Qal'at er-Rabad, above Ajlun. Built by one of Saladin's emirs in A.D. 1184, it was destroyed by Mongol invaders in A.D. 1260, rebuilt shortly thereafter by Sultan Baybars, and occupied as late as the 19th century A.D. by Ibrahim Pasha.

Photo by Nelson Glueck

FIG. 53. Yarmuk River.

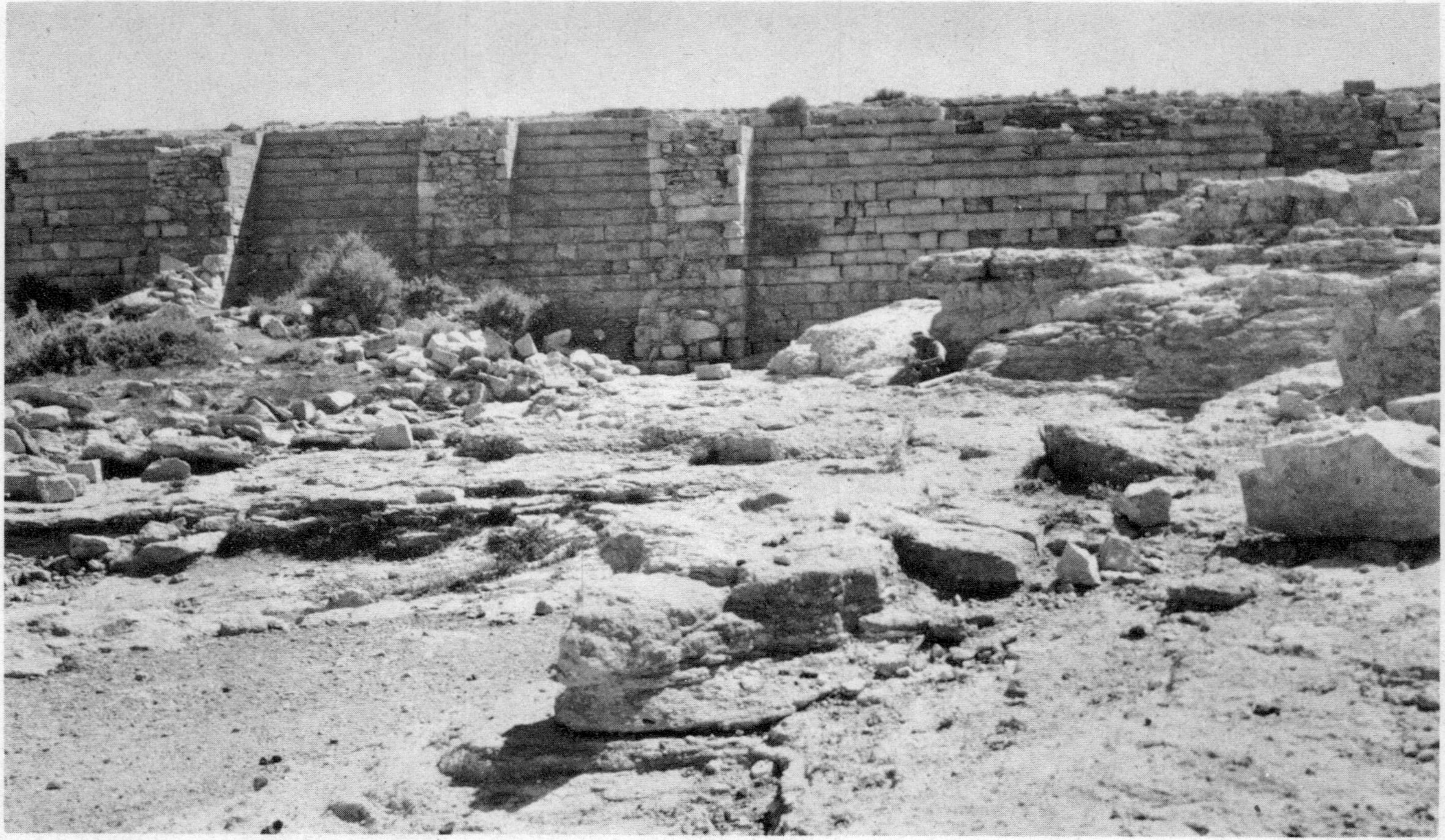

FIG. 54. Roman dam in Wadi Dhobai in Transjordan desert.

was under him went away" (ch. 18:9). In this position he was found, and the darts that David's general, Joab, thrust through the heart of the hapless youth were in effect to pierce also the heart of his father when the news was conveyed to him. What had he further to hope for, as he sat between the gates of Mahanaim hugging his grief to his bosom. Aged, bereft of a dearly beloved, if wayward, son, whose violence had been after the manner of his own father, had it not been better if the son had lived, and David through death had found expiation and peace? "O my son Absalom, my son, my son Absalom! would I had died for thee, O Absalom, my son, my son!" (v. 33). But as surely as the Jabbok by which he raised his lament flowed into the Jordan, and the Jordan into the Sea of Death, so inevitable, David brooded, had been the consequences of his living, the death of his hope. "O Absalom, my son, my son!"

<h1 style="text-align:center">7</h1>

What sights an ancient land sees during the centuries and what stories its stones could tell! Listen! Whence came these unbridled lamentations that tear the silence from the sides of the Jabbok canyon? What searing sadness has burned laughter from women's lips and made them shriek endlessly, with a yielding more unrestrained to sorrow than to a passionate embrace? And then, suddenly, singing! Sweet singing, swelling fiercely, subsiding sadly, followed by clamorous silence. What frightful fate has befallen a fellow mortal? Bursting through the thicket into an open meadow on top of a high hill, which from time immemorial had been devoted to divinity, we behold a group of maidens gathered around—yes, now we know— gathered round the daughter of Jephthah! The dread tale has been bruited about. Quickly, now, back into the woods before being observed! And away, hasten away, and leave them to strip their sorrow naked in solitude! Never shall we forget the tall, slim virgin, winningly robed in deathless white, standing frozen, silent, in the midst of her company!

Below, far below, ran the waters of the Jabbok to the Jordan. It was because of her father's war for the security of the Jabbok, and the safety of Israel, that Jephthah's daughter was to die. What grievous burden to lay on soft shoulders that no lover's hand had yet caressed, nor now would ever touch! This had happened before the prophet said: "Every one shall die for his own iniquity: every man that eateth sour grapes, his teeth shall be set on edge" (Jer. 31:30; Ezek. 18:2). In vain had Jephthah attempted to dissuade the king of Ammon from seizing territory not his on the basis of trumped-up historical allegations. Insistently had he urged him to remember that the lands he now demanded had been held by Israel for three hundred years, without its claim ever being questioned. Long ago, in fair fight with Sihon, king of the Amorites, who had denied Israel access through his territory to the Jordan, Israel had come into possession of "all the border of the Amorites, from the Arnon unto the Jabbok, and from the wilderness even unto the Jordan" (Judg. 11:22). But when have men of violence listened to words of wisdom? "Howbeit the king of Bene-Ammon hearkened not unto the words of Jephthah which he sent him" (v. 28). So Jephthah made ready for war.

Fierce soul of simple sentiment, he made a vow that if he emerged victorious from the impending battle he would give as a gift to God the very first thing he saw when he got home again—and he was thinking of one of his fat sheep or heavy bulls of Bashan. Assured thus in his heart of divine intervention in his behalf, "Jephthah passed over unto the Bene-Ammon to fight against them. . . . And he smote them, . . . so that the Bene-Ammon were subdued before the Bene-Israel" (vs. 32, 33). His duty done, Jephthah hastened to his home at Mizpah in Gilead. Now, he thought, rubbing his hands in pleasurable anticipation as he neared his dwelling, which of his animals would be the first to cross his path to be served as a sacrifice to his success? And then the castle of his glee collapsed and his heart was crushed within him. Running to meet the grizzled warrior was his carefree, dearly beloved daughter, about whom his own life revolved. The news of his coming had outsped him. Panting for his appearance, this only child of his had run like a gazelle to be the first of his family to reach him. Now indeed he was undone by Ammon, and by his own primitive faith from which he knew no retreat.

"And Jephthah came to Mizpah unto his house; and, behold, his daughter came out to meet him with timbrels and with dances. She was his only child; besides her he had neither son nor daughter. And it came to pass, when he saw her, that he rent his clothes, and said, Alas, my daughter! thou hast brought me very low, and thou art one of them that trouble me; for I have opened my mouth unto the Lord, and I cannot go back" (vs. 34, 35). No cry of consternation from the warrior-daughter! No pitiful plea for retraction of the perverse promise! "And she said unto him, My father, thou hast opened thy mouth unto the Lord; do unto me according to that which proceeded out of thy mouth, inasmuch as the Lord hath taken vengeance for thee on thine enemies, even on the Bene-Ammon. And she said unto her father, Let this thing be done for me: let me alone for two months, that I may depart and go down upon the mountains, and bewail my virginity, I and my companions. And he said, Go. . . .And it came to pass at the end of two months, that she returned unto her father, who did with her according to his vow which he had vowed: and she knew not man. And it was a custom in Israel, that the daughters of Israel went yearly to celebrate the daughter of Jephthah the Gileadite four days in a year" (vs. 36–40).

Where was her retreat in the mountains? On a wind-swept height overlooking the steep descent to the River Jabbok is a small, tumbledown stone structure, standing close to a gnarled oak tree. In the crevices of the building, and hanging from the branches of the tree, are pitiful little rags and bits of string, placed there by poor pilgrims in token of fervent vows. Such are their offerings to the god of nature, long considered resident on this commanding hilltop. It matters not that the worshipers are superficially Moslems, who profess adherence to one God, Allah, and who incline according to the instructions of his prophet, Mohammed. The patrons of this sanctuary are pagans, by whatever name they may be known. With humility and wonder in their hearts, they beat difficult ways to the shrine of an ancient god, whose manner is dim in their memories, but whose hold is strong on their souls. I like to think that it was to this high place, once green with woods, overlooking the Jabbok

River from the south, that the daughter of Jephthah and her companions retired, and the maidens of Israel for long thereafter repaired, to wail over her untimely death.

At this juncture in his life, how ill-advised of the men of Ephraim to offer affront to Jephthah! They dared raise angry accusation against him, because, forsooth, he had fought the Ammonites without them. Raucous voices shrilled vehement invective, all the more vicious because of underlying falsehood. In truth he had called them to help, but receiving no reply had acted independently while there was yet time. Was this the hero's reward? Was boundless insult to be heaped now upon his fathomless sorrow? His sacrifice had, after all, saved them too! In this hour of his heaviness of heart they had actually taken up arms against him. They were even threatening to burn down his house, the house in which Jephthah's daughter had once sat and sung! To his undying credit be it said that Jephthah remonstrated with these ingrates of Ephraim, who had become brave when victory was won. Unable, however, to dissuade them, he attacked their camp at Zaphon on the east side of the Jordan Valley, to which they had come from their western hills. So thoroughly were they defeated that no refuge was left even for straggling fugitives. The few who, in disguise, sought to recross the Jordan betrayed themselves by their peculiar accent to Jephthah's guards stationed at its fords.

The Bible has graphically recorded this entire incident: "And the men of Ephraim were gathered together, and passed over to Zaphon; and they said unto Jephthah, Wherefore passedst thou over to fight against the Bene-Ammon, and didst not call us to go with thee?. . . And Jephthah said unto them, I and my people were at great strife with the Bene-Ammon. When I called unto you, ye saved me not out of their hand. And when I saw that ye saved me not, I put my life in my hand, and passed over against the Bene-Ammon, and the Lord delivered them into my hand: wherefore then are ye come up unto me this day to fight against me? Then Jephthah gathered together all the men of Gilead, and . . . smote Ephraim, . . . and . . . took the fords of the Jordan against the Ephraimites. And it was so, that, when any of the fugitives of Ephraim said, Let me go over, the men of

Photo by Govt. of Palestine, Dept. of Antiquities

Fig. 55. Reservoir at Umm el-Jemal, first built in Nabataean-Roman times, still sufficiently watertight to hold the seasonal rain water, although the site itself has for centuries been empty of inhabitants.

Photo by Nelson Glueck

FIG. 56. Underground reservoir at Beit Ras, Transjordan, the site of ancient Capitolias.

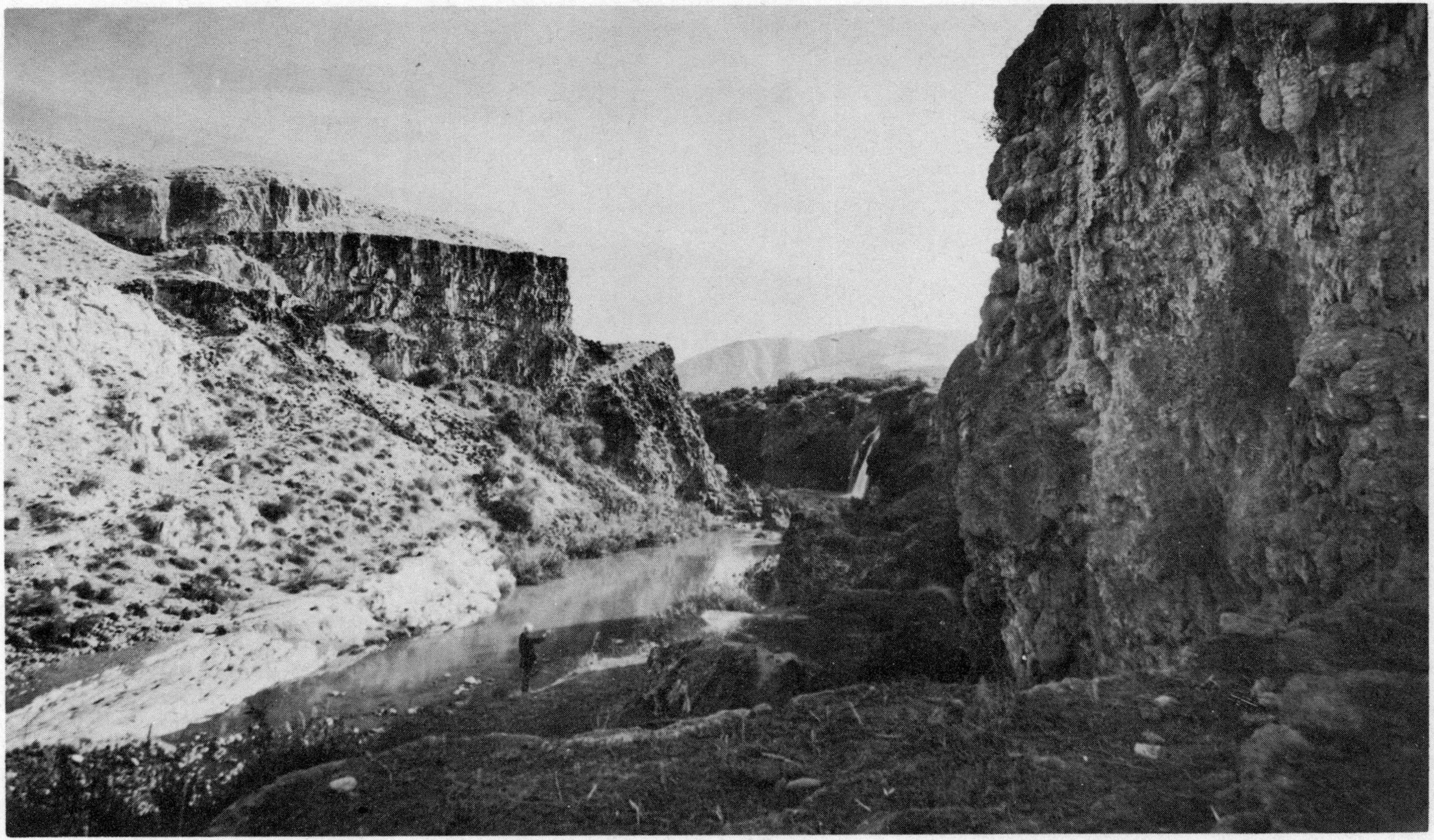

FIG. 57. Yarmuk River, showing waterfall of Mekheibeh.

Photo by Govt. of Palestine, Dept. of Antiquities

FIG. 58. The Moslem Dome of the Rock, seen behind the city wall of Jerusalem, whose lower courses belong to the time of Herod the Great.

Gilead said unto him, . . . Say now Shibboleth; and he said Sibboleth; for he could not frame to pronounce it right: in such an instance they took hold of him, and slew him at the fords of the Jordan'' (ch. 12: 1–6).

8

Where was Zaphon? Among the many ancient sites, whose ruins remain in the Jordan Valley, which is to be identified with Zaphon? The modern names of these places give no hint of their original designations. Only through their present prefixes *tell* (artificial city mound, concealing within it the debris of many settlements piled one over the other) and *khirbeh* (ruin) do they vaguely reveal the fact of former habitation. These forgotten heaps of debris, piled at times hill-high, were once groups of houses vibrant with human sounds. Village elders deliberated in the gateways; the hubbub of traffic filled the air. Now, merely sad symbols of snuffed-out life, the ruins are sought out by tent dwellers as burial grounds for their dead, or, being raised above the moist valley floor, are used to house dry grain pits, where surplus wheat and barley are cannily stored. Vague references, however, give important clues. Fragments of pottery, more indestructible than stone, are eloquent of the time of their construction and the manner of the civilization in which the pottery was produced. Contours of country, sources of water, and routes of travel are among other factors that help to rediscover ancient sites. In such wise Zaphon has been identified with Tell Qos.

Tell Qos, in the Jordan Valley, is on a high, flat-topped, completely isolated hill, on the north side of the River Rajeb, near its outlet from the eastern hills. It commands a splendid view over much of the valley, and over the course of the Wadi Rajeb westward toward its junction with the Jordan. It is an obvious strategic center on an important crossroads, one branch of which leads up into the hills of Gilead, where Mizpah, the home of Jephthah, lay. The masters of Tell Qos were in a position to give or withhold permission to use the waters of the Rajeb stream, and held thus the welfare of the farmers of the district in their hands. Agriculture was possible only through irrigation. The Rajeb is north of the River Jabbok, and, according to the Bible, Zaphon is the first important district center on the east side of the valley, north of Succoth (which is located near the entrance of the Jabbok into the Jordan Valley). Tell Qos is the only site which can be equated with Zaphon.

The early age of Zaphon is indicated by its very name, which shows that it was a sanctuary of Baal-zaphon, long worshiped before being displaced by devotion to invisible Jehovah. When I climbed to the top of Tell Qos one day to map its ruins and collect the fragments of pottery strewn on its surface, which reveal the various ages of its occupation, some of which go back to more than 3,000 years before the time of Christ, I saw a madman sitting there. I tried to talk to him, but could not tear him from his contemplation. I wondered what were his connections with the past.

The loudmouthed Ephraimites had finally been taught a lesson they should long previously have learned. On an earlier occasion, Gideon of Abiezer had had to contend with them, because, without waiting for their aid, he had delivered Israel from Midianite oppression. Then too the men of Ephraim had upbraided their savior for the victory he had won for them. "And the men of Ephraim said unto him, Why hast thou served us thus, that thou calledst us not, when thou wentest to fight with Midian? And they did chide him sharply. And he said unto them, What have I now done in comparison with you? Is not the gleaning of the grapes of Ephraim better than the vintage of Abiezer?. . . Then their anger was abated toward him" (Judg. 8:1–3).

9

The Midianites and other Bedouins were wont at harvest time to make rapid raids across the Jordan, carry off the crops of Israel from the very threshing floors, and drive off whatever livestock they could lay their hands on. The struggle between the Desert and the Sown is continuous. Hungry nomads have ever pressed into plowed lands, content to take by swift violence what others have gained by hard toil. When Gideon was summoned to head off the raiders, he "was

beating out wheat in the winepress, to hide it from the Midianites"
(ch. 6:11). Gideon and his band dispersed the Bedouins, who re-
treated eastward across the Jordan. Inflicting severe punishment
upon them, they pursued them hotly into and beyond the hills of
Gilead, until finally the raiders lost themselves in the reaches of the
desert.

On the way through the Jordan Valley and up the hard path
climbing to the top of the Jabbok canyon, Gideon and his troops
had been ill received by the men of Succoth and Penuel. He had
promised himself and them to repay their conduct in kind once the
chase was over. "And Gideon . . . returned from the battle, . . . and
catching hold of a lad from Succoth, he pressed him to write down
the names of seventy-seven of the princes and elders of Succoth"
(ch. 8:13, 14). In his hour of need they had refused to give bread to
his men, who were faint from hunger, so now Gideon "took the
elders of the city, and thorns of the wilderness and briers, and with
them he taught the men of Succoth. And he [also] broke down the
tower of Penuel, and slew the men of the city" (vs. 16, 17).

IO

Stranger scenes than these, however, had been enacted still earlier
on the banks of the Jabbok, as it flowed by the sites of Penuel and
Succoth on its way to the Jordan. Had not one of the patriarchs seen
God face to face at Penuel? Jacob was returning from his long sojourn in Mesopotamia, where he had acquired a large family and
much substance in service with his father-in-law, Laban. He had fled
to that far-off land originally to escape the wrath of his brother Esau,
whose rights as first-born he had bought for a mess of pottage, and
whose blessing as first-born he had obtained by trickery from their
blind father. Twenty years had elapsed since then, and now Jacob's
face turned homeward. The nearer he came, the sharper the conflict
in his own soul. He hesitated to cross the Jabbok. Inner torment
gave him no peace. The years had not killed his fear of Esau's anger.
The voice of his conscience had been no more silenced than the flow
of the Jabbok had ceased. He had wronged his father; he had robbed

his brother. Would punishment finally catch up with him? Would he ever be able again to cross the Jordan and live the rest of his life on his native heath?

"And he rose up that night, and took his two wives, and . . . his eleven children, and passed over the ford of the Jabbok. And he took them, and sent them over the stream, and all that which he had. And Jacob was left alone; and there wrestled a man with him until the breaking of the day. And when he saw that he prevailed not against him, he touched the hollow of his thigh; and the hollow of Jacob's thigh was strained, as he wrestled with him. And he said, Let me go, for the day breaketh. And he replied, I will not let thee go, except thou bless me. Whereupon he said unto him, What is thy name? And he said, Jacob. And he said, Thy name shall be no more called Jacob, but Israel [he who striveth with God]: for thou hast striven with God and with men, and hast prevailed. . . . And he blessed him there. And Jacob called the name of the place Penuel [the face of God]: for, he said, I have seen God face to face, and my life is preserved. And the sun rose upon him as he passed over Penuel, and he limped upon his thigh. Therefore the children of Israel eat not the sinew of the hip which is upon the hollow of the thigh, unto this day: because he touched the hollow of Jacob's thigh" (Gen. 32:22–32).

I have slept out overnight on Tell edh-Dhahab (the "Hill of Gold"), which is probably to be identified with Penuel. The canyon walls widen out considerably at this point, as the hills, through which the Jabbok cuts its way, begin to tumble down toward their meeting place with the Jordan Valley. The rushing little stream bends around the base of this hill on three sides, and in flood season cuts it off altogether from the mainland, as if to say, "This is a particularly important place, not to be associated with the ordinary mundane world." From the top of the hill there is a good view over the Jordan Valley and across it to the hills of Palestine. Some sense of sanctity still hovers over this place. My Arab companions were very loath to have me sleep there alone, but would on no condition accompany me there to spend the night. They made their camp at the foot of the hill, warning me that if I persisted in my intention to sleep

FIG. 59. The Temple area in Jerusalem, showing the Dome of the Rock, and the el-ʿAqsa mosque behind it.

FIG. 60. Qeseir 'Amra, an 8th century A.D. Umaiyad hunting lodge
in the desert in eastern Transjordan.

Photo by Govt. of Palestine, Dept. of Antiquities

FIG. 61. Interior of 8th century A.D. Umaiyad castle at Amman, Transjordan.

Photo by Govt. of Palestine, Dept. of Antiquities

FIG. 62. Detail of inner wall of 8th century A.D. Umaiyad castle at Amman, Transjordan.

on top of it, a spirit (jinni) would seize me during the night, and that if indeed I did survive the ordeal I would wake up in the morning *majnun*, that is, possessed by the spirit. But here Jacob had wrestled during the night with his Adversary, being left alone only at the break of dawn. And here I would sleep or sit out the night, with the living past breathing its vivid tale into my ears. What would happen to me before I crossed the Jordan again? What are those sounds? The sighs of Jacob, the accents of Esau? Dawn had come. My Arabs had been shouting to me to come down, concerned for my safety.

Inwardly purified, Jacob made ready to meet his brother. His fears proved to be in vain. Esau accepted his gifts and forgave the crime committed against him. "And Jacob lifted up his eyes, and looked, and, behold, Esau was coming, and with him four hundred men. . . . And Esau ran to meet him, and embraced him, and fell on his neck, and kissed him: and they wept" (ch. 33:1–4). Long they talked, neither at first quite convinced of the other's intentions, till at last, in complete reconciliation, they parted again, each going his own way. "So Esau returned that day on his way to Seir. And Jacob journeyed to Succoth, and built him a house, and made booths for his cattle: therefore the name of the place is called Succoth [Booths]" (vs. 16, 17). What a magnificent site Succoth occupies near the entrance of the Jabbok into the Jordan Valley, where it is unquestionably to be identified with Tell Deir'alla. But more about that anon.

I I

The most important tributary of the Jordan north of the Jabbok is the River Yarmuk, which ran through the territory of the fabulous Og, king of Bashan. He was the last of the Rephaim, the Giants, who according to Biblical tradition, together with Sihon, the other king of the Amorites, ruled the territory in Transjordan extending from the Arnon as far as Mount Hermon, north of the Yarmuk. After Og's death, his gigantic bed was put on exhibition at Rabbath Ammon, and mobs of sightseers viewed it with wonder. Unfortunately it has not endured down to this day. "His [Og's] bed was a bed of iron. Is it not on display at Rabbath of the Bene-Ammon, nine

cubits in length, and four in width, according to the cubit of a man?"
(Deut. 3:11). Og had two residences, one in Ashtaroth and another
at Edrei, both in the Yarmuk basin. The one, long abandoned, is still
known as Tell Ashtarah, and the other as Der'ah, today an important
railway junction. The railway line from Haifa branches off there
northeast to Damascus and south to Amman. Der'ah or Edrei has
apparently been occupied more or less continuously for at least five
thousand years. Among its wonders is a complete subterranean city,
which hails back mainly to Roman and Byzantine times. The wadi,
or stream bed, below it drains into the Yarmuk, which is fed by a
considerable number of small tributaries coming from northern
Gilead and southern Syria.

Standing on the edge of the fertile plateau of north Gilead, and
looking down into the depths of the mighty chasm of the Yarmuk
(Fig. 53), one would scarcely count on finding any ancient settlements along its narrow banks or precipitous slopes. So impelling,
however, has population pressure been in the lands bordering the inhospitable spaces of the desert of Arabia that no area at all arable has
been left untouched. Even marginal lands were put into cultivation.
Were one to estimate in terms of financial return on labor and capital
investment, as such things are reckoned today, the cost of estab-
lishing and maintaining a village on one of the sides or at the bottom
of the Yarmuk gorge, or in regions even less favorable for human
dwelling, it would seem hopelessly impractical. But the ancients
never figured that way. They labored for the sake of survival.

The Nabataeans in Transjordan, during the first centuries B.C. and
A.D., by building reservoirs and dams, saved every possible drop of
water, and by constructing terraces preserved the soil from destruc-
tive erosion. Thus they were able to wrest an existence even out of
the grim depths of the Wadi Arabah, at places like et-Tlah, which
had never previously been inhabited. Like the Nabataeans, the Romans, and later the Byzantines, established in semiarid areas large
towns which are almost completely uninhabited today, although the
climate has not changed. The economic life of these towns was based
on dry farming, on herds of sheep, goats, and camels, and on trade.

In parts of southern Palestine, where the rainfall is inadequate for agriculture, dams and cisterns were built, and cities throve for several centuries. Even in the wastes of eastern Transjordan the Romans built dams in places like the Wadi Dhobai to catch the freshets caused by occasional rains, and thus provide water for numerous flocks (Fig. 54). Visit the forbidding lands of northernmost Transjordan, and see a whole series of ruins which were flourishing towns in Nabataean-Roman-Byzantine times. Almost each house had a covered cistern, hewn out of solid rock and at least ten feet square and deep. Each town had several large reservoirs (Figs. 55, 56). The sight of the massive ruins in this area between the Iraq Petroleum Company's pipe line and the Syrian border, such as Umm el-Jemal, Sabhah, Deir el-Kahf, Umm el-Qetein, and Burqa'ah, leaves one filled with amazement at what men can accomplish when peace and vision, planning and perseverance, common need and productive co-operation, prevail.

To those who escape from the penury of the desert, the pain of the plowman is of little account if the result be a larger amount of food or any improvement whatsoever in their own and their children's welfare. Wherever in the Near East I have found water—it matters not how rugged the terrain, how unfriendly the soil—there I have found traces of ancient civilizations, and sometimes a continuous record of settlement from the earliest historical times. Thus it is that not only on the top of the plateau of Gilead, which overlooks the Yarmuk from the south and where the fairest lands of all Transjordan may be found, but even in the depths of the Yarmuk gorge, I have found remains of ancient settlements, large and small, early and late, eloquent of man's creative activity, and of his frenzied attachment to the soil.

Westward the Yarmuk flows through a canyon grim with volcanic blackness (Fig. 57), pouring finally into the Jordan at a point about 4 miles south of the Lake of Galilee. In its final stage, it passes through a rich plain, which becomes part of the Jordan Valley. It comes to the Jordan on equal terms, being, like it, 30 feet broad at the place of union.

FIG. 63. (*a*)—A magnificent mosaic from the 8th century A.D. Umaiyad castle of Khirbet Mefjer, several miles north of Jericho. It shows a stylized pomegranate (?) tree, with a lion attacking one of three gazelles grazing underneath its branches. The border surrounding this brilliantly hued mosaic gives it a tapestrylike effect. To achieve a sense of depth, the leaves of the tree are depicted in colors ranging from leaf green to yellowish green to blue gray. The branches and trunk are in various shades of brown; the animals in shades of pale yellow to coffee brown; the border in red, white, and black.

FIG. 63. (*b*)—Stucco panel of busts from the 8th century A.D. Umaiyad castle of Khirbet Mefjer, near Jericho.

120

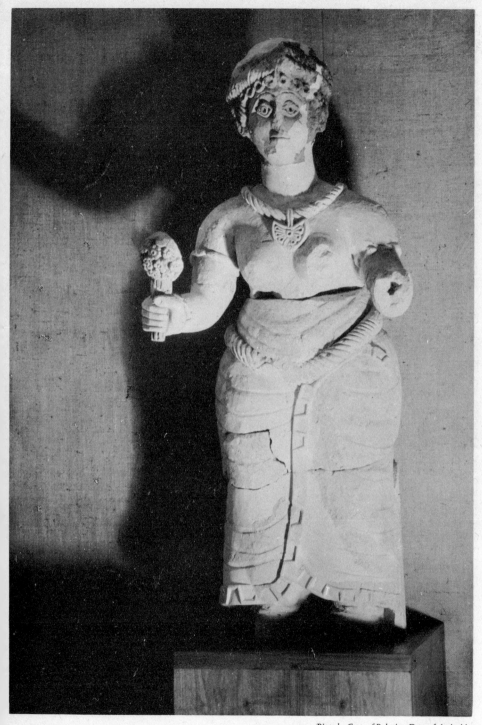

FIG. 64. Stucco statue of girl with flowers, from Khirbet Mefjer, north of Jericho, where the Umaiyads, early Mohammedan Arabs, built a resplendent palace in the 8th century A.D.

FIG. 65. Stucco figure of helmeted man, from Khirbet Mefjer.

FIG. 66. Stucco figure of fox (?) eating grapes, from Khirbet Mefjer.

12

It was through the Yarmuk gorge that the Arab flood cascaded down into the Jordan Valley, after overwhelming the army of Heraclius. Within a few short years it inundated all of Palestine. Jerusalem opened its gates to the Caliph Omar in A.D. 637, and Caesarea was conquered in A.D. 640. A new era ensued, at first a beneficent one. The Umaiyad and Abbasid caliphs brought many blessings to the entire Near East. They were among the last in that part of the world who paid careful attention to the cultivation of the soil, to the building up of terraces, and to the construction and repair of dams, reservoirs, and aqueducts. They learned much about art and architecture from their predecessors, but soon progressed beyond them.

What better tribute to the architectural accomplishments of these Umaiyads can there be, for instance, than the magnificent Dome of the Rock (Fig. 58) and the Mosque el-'Aqsa in Jerusalem (Fig. 59), built (with the aid of Greek Christian architects and workmen) in A.D. 691 by the Umaiyad prince, 'Abd el-Malik? And who has traveled in the eastern deserts of Transjordan and not been amazed by the beauty of the hunting lodges which Arab princes erected there to while away some weeks of leisure during the spring of the year? To a place such as Qeseir 'Amra in the Transjordan desert (Fig. 60) they could return after a day's hunting, and further amuse themselves with poetry and astronomy, as well as with wine, women, and song. Reclining on their couches, they would gaze on ceilings decorated with paintings of fat nudes and of dancing bears playing musical instruments.

The ruins of a beautiful Umaiyad structure are visible in Amman (Figs. 61, 62). On the northwest shore of the Lake of Galilee, at Khirbet Minyeh, the remains of an Umaiyad castle have been discovered. It is immediately south of et-Tabghah, where is located the Byzantine church with the mosaic depicting the five loaves and two fishes with which Jesus fed the five thousand. And a most elaborate winter palace, built by the Umaiyads, has been partly excavated at Khirbet Mefjer, 3 miles north of Jericho (Figs. 63–66). It was destroyed before completion by an earthquake in the middle of the eighth century A.D. Its dimensions and general plan, its sculptures and decorations, exhibit Umaiyad art to high advantage, and show an ultimate connection with the Oriental art of the Hellenized Nabataeans. These early Umaiyads, too, are thus among the long line of those who have left a mark on the Jordan Valley.

FIG. 67. A dolmen overlooking the Plains of Moab.

V

Mountain Streams and Valley Cities:
The Lower Basin

1

BETWEEN the Lake of Galilee and the Sea of Salt, there are, on the east side of the Jordan, eleven perennial streams which cut their way from the eastern hills down to the Jordan. They water the valley into the greenness which made Lot call it a garden of God. Their names sound strange to the unaccustomed ear, but water spells music and wealth in any language. Between the Yarmuk and Jabbok the Rivers Arab, Ziqlab, Jurm, Yabis, Kufrinji, and Rajeb flow all year round. Beyond them, south of the Jabbok, are the Nimrin, Kefrein, and Rameh. The Wadi Azeimeh empties into the Dead Sea. All of them hew their lines through the hills as though with a mighty ax. The Biblical names of most of these streams elude us. The knowledge of their existence, however, makes understandable the fact that the Jordan Valley was the home of some of the very earliest settlements of man anywhere in the Near East.

2

Between the Jabbok and the Nimrin on the east side of the Jordan is an arid region about sixteen miles long, with neither springs nor streams to moisten its dryness. Its acres could not be made productive in the past, and people had no reason to congregate in towns, or hope for survival if they did. Rain occurs only in occasional years. When it does fall, the short-lived grass, which springs up magically in its wake, is quickly cropped to its roots by hungry flocks of Bedouins' sheep and goats. Stone circles, revealing the tenting places of such shepherds, go back in part to high antiquity. For many long centuries the land there was vacant, in sharp contrast to the once populous and intensively tilled parts of the Jordan Valley north and south of it.

This condition was changed in small part when the dynamic Romans came along, and the push of growing populations in the Near East became so strong that every available inch of ground had to be utilized if at all possible. I estimate, on the basis of hundreds of ancient sites discovered by our archaeological survey, that the population in Transjordan during the Roman and equally populous Byzantine periods amounted to about a million and a quarter, compared to the present urban to nomadic 350,000. In those days, as we have seen, the soil was sacred. It was tended with a loving care that helped to preserve it from one generation to another. Hillsides were terraced at the cost of great toil. Forests, which covered large stretches of the country, were carefully preserved, with conscious or unconscious concern for their irreplaceable values. Dams (Fig. 54), reservoirs (Fig. 55), and cisterns without number (Fig. 56) were built to conserve the available water supply. Aqueducts spanned the land. Even underground water supplies were tapped.

The Romans did not despair of utilizing part of the desert section of the Jordan Valley between the Jabbok and the Nimrin streams. At one point, someone noticed a small trickle of water at the bottom of the gentle slope which led across the valley from the base of the hills on its east side. A ditch was dug following the course of the seepage of water, and the farther the ditch went the greater was the quantity of water obtained. Soon the ditch was too deep to be continued without its walls collapsing, or without widening it, which apparently proved to be impractical. By that time, it had evidently occurred to the venturesome engineer in charge of operations that he had struck an underground water table. He proceeded to have a series of vertical shafts dug down to the water table, and these were connected by a tunnel with each other and with the ditch previously dug. Thus, at the bottom of each shaft, a certain amount of water was collected from the spongy earth about it. The water flowed then by gravity through the tunnel to the bottom of the next shaft slightly below it, and so on, till finally it emerged into the ditch as a strong stream, capable of irrigating numerous fields. All that was necessary thereafter was to keep the tunnel and the shafts that led into it free of debris. No hoisting or pumping was necessary. Imagine the elation of the engineer who first pioneered this project. Water obtained in the desert by striking its rock!

Only recently, the engineers of Emir Abdullah, the titular ruler of Transjordan, rediscovered this artesian system. Someone noticed the same trickle of water that attracted the attention of the Roman engineer, and at the same time observed a long line of filled-in pits leading down the gentle slope from east to west. The pits were cleared, the interconnecting tunnel found and opened, and the whole system restored to use. Gardens now flourish in this desert, where no cultivated plants have thrived since the Byzantine period. Similar artesian wells, known today as *qanat* or *fuqara*, have been found elsewhere in the Near East, all of them hailing back to Roman and Byzantine times. Little wonder then that the Bible says nothing of this parched area on the east side of the Jordan Valley. During the Nabataean, Roman, and Byzantine periods, between particularly the second century B.C. and the sixth century A.D., dynamic populations pushed out into marginal lands, where no permanent, sedentary civilizations preceded or followed them. By skillful and persistent conservation of occasional rain water, and where possible by wise cultivation and care of the soil, they were able to survive, often even to flourish, in arid and semiarid areas, which have for long since then been practically empty of settled inhabitants.

3

I have examined archaeologically some seventy ancient sites on the east side of the Jordan Valley, the presence of most of which was previously unknown. Over half of the number can be dated to the Israelite period, beginning about the thirteenth century B.C. The Biblical editors were probably familiar with the locations of most of these sites, as well as with their histories and traditions, yet they mentioned only nine of them. Why then did they fail to describe or even list all of them in their records? Indeed the very paucity of names of Biblical sites in the Jordan Valley has helped to give currency to the notion that it was largely abandoned in Biblical times. It has been thought that it was used then mainly for grazing, being visited only during the planting and harvesting seasons in the early spring and late summer.

The explanation is not far to seek. For the Bible to have mentioned every one of the thirty-five or more Israelite places dating between the thirteenth and sixth centuries B.C. which have been discovered now on the east side of the Jordan Valley alone, would have been contrary to the method and purpose of its editors. They were neither interested in furnishing a Baedeker list of all towns in any given district nor in writing a historical geography of the Holy Land or an onomasticon of Palestine. For them, all history was subsumed under religion. They culled materials from source books such as the Book of Jashar in order to elaborate the thesis which pervades every page of Sacred Writ, that God is One and Good, that he is the God of history, and that all men are his children. In addition, they were much too shrewd storytellers to burden their record with a multiplicity of unnecessary names.

4

Long before the Bible was composed, perhaps even before writing was invented, civilized life was stirring in the Jordan Valley and in the hills and plains above it. Man made tools and weapons of flint, and built houses and tombs, called dolmens, of huge slabs of stone (Fig. 67). These monuments raised by the dolmen builders have made their memory endure for some 7,500 years, more or less, and they may easily last for another ten millenniums. Otherwise, little is known of these ancient men whose skill enabled them to quarry and move by hand great stone blocks which today would require heavy machinery to lift. One thing is certain, that the architects of these structures were not primitive troglodytes who burrowed for shelter in caves, nor simple shepherds who dwelt only in tents. They were experienced craftsmen and farmers trained in the skills of their day. It hardly seems possible that they lived so long ago.

FIG. 68. A dolmen in the foothills east of Tell Damieh (Biblical Adamah), with an aperture in what was originally a middle partition.

Photo by Royal Air Force, Levant

FIG. 69. The Jabbok on the right nearing the point of its junction with the Jordan on the left. In between them may be seen the whitish, eroded marl hills leading up to the higher, *Ghor* level of the Jordan Valley, which at this point narrows down to a pointed tongue as the two rivers begin to come together. At the southern tip of this tongue of the *Ghor* is the whitish patch of the double Kh. Umm Hamad site, the east part of which existed as a flourishing agricultural settlement in the 4th millennium B.C.

Photo by American Schools of Oriental Research

FIG. 70. Fourth millennium B.C. broken lattice-burnished jar from Khirbet Umm Hamad Sherqi in the Jordan Valley.

FIG. 71. Goatskins are used today in the Jordan Valley for water containers, instead of the graceful pottery jars anciently employed.

134

Look! Is not that a group of them, standing on the slope of a hill above the east side of the Jordan Valley? There below, in the distance, is the line of the Jabbok converging with that of the Jordan! Several men are examining a vertical outcrop of limestone, studying its seams and its grain! "Yes, this will do," they seem to say. Wooden wedges are inserted, powerful arms wield heavy stone hammers, and soon a mighty slab is broken off, measuring perhaps 7 feet long, 5 feet wide, and 2 feet thick. In slow succession, three others of approximately similar size are prepared, and then two smaller ones. Meanwhile, another group of workmen has been building a circular platform of stone blocks, which rises in several narrowing stages to a flat top. The great slabs are now tipped and turned over again and again till they are brought to the base of the platform, and then, on rollers, pushed and pulled up a dirt incline to its top. These people understand the principles of leverage! Sweat pours freely from their faces, and the strain makes the veins on their arms and foreheads stand out, but still it is careful skill rather than brute force which makes it possible to move these megaliths. One of the stones is laid flat, two others are set up lengthwise on their narrow sides, three feet apart from each other, and then another great stone laid over them as a roof (Fig. 68). Now the tomb is ready for its occupant! The funeral procession approaches, and the body is inserted, together with a few flint tools and some food for the long journey into the afterlife. Then the ends are sealed with smaller slabs. Now everyone joins in the work, and a mound of dirt is heaped over the massive cairn. Farewell, dear departed!

Who among the mourners could know that long, very long after your bones have disintegrated into dust, your gravestones will still be standing? But your sleep will not remain undisturbed for long. Human moles will burrow into your bed to seize the few possessions buried with you. Several thousand years later, your kind will have been wiped off the face of the earth, and other men of different groups will have lain, each in his turn and period, in your place. The process will often be repeated. Down through the ages, your last dwelling will house new corpses from passing populations. The day will come when Roman and Byzantine pottery will be found on the dolmen's floor.

At the edge of the valley, on the hills and plateau above it, and on the slopes in between, I have seen these dolmens by their hundreds and thousands, littering the entire length of Transjordan. Dolmen fields stretch north into Syria, and west into Palestine. Their builders belonged to a people so numerous that many of them spilled over into marginal lands, where at least flocks could be maintained if crops could not be cultivated. They apparently worked separate farms, and lived in long, narrow, thick-walled houses, resembling the dolmens. High in the hills of Transjordan, near the modern Arabic village of Kefr Kifya, I stumbled across the remains of what I believe to be one of their massive houses. Its two long walls are still standing, made of rude flint blocks, with small chunks of stone between them. It measured 33 feet long, 25 feet wide, and was probably originally about 6 feet high. Each wall is about 7 feet thick. Over them at one time was a roof, made perhaps of wooden beams. Even if this should prove not to be one of their houses, can the thought be sensibly entertained that the men who built dolmen tombs, some of them two stories high or two chambers broad, or two chambers long with a connecting aperture, could not or would not have built homes for the living?

What catastrophe overcame these early inhabitants of the Jordan Valley and the neighboring lands? Perhaps they suffered the fate which was to be the common lot of all their successors. Living on the fringe of the desert and constantly exposed to the forays of the Bedouins, they were finally overwhelmed. The newcomers who took their places were transformed in time into tillers of the soil. And new nomads dispossessed them in turn. Horites and Amorites, Aramaeans and Israelites, Nabataeans and Arabs, Crusaders and Mongols invaded the land and remained to farm its fields. Each time hundreds or possibly thousands of natives were massacred, and other thousands were driven away. Always, however, a large number remained, often to enslave their new masters, partially or completely, by giving them their gods and their blood, although not always their knowledge and attainments. The only physical things that have remained permanent in the Jordan Valley are the flow of the Jordan and its tributaries, and the comparative fertility of the soil on either side of it, conditioned as they are by the country's physical geography. Split in two by the fateful river, and strait-jacketed between the Mediterranean Sea on the west and the desert on the east and south, this narrow strip of land, "flowing with milk and honey," has been continuously coveted and frequently conquered by strangers.

5

If one can imagine a spotlight moving across a darkened stage of history, illuminating past periods and places, it might be considered as lighting up next the peninsulalike projection of the Jordan Valley caught between the junction of the Jabbok and Jordan Rivers (Fig. 69). The light now brings a very large town out of the blackness. Square-built, flat-roofed, mud-brick houses become visible, with narrow lanes threading between them. There is a kiln, with rows of pots arranged in front of it, some already baked and ready for use! Look at that pottery, you connoisseurs! Are not these the types in use during most of the last five hundred years of the fourth millennium before Christ was born (and belonging, in terms of scientific jargon, to the Upper Chalcolithic and Early Bronze I periods)? The spotlight has turned away! I should like to have seen more. Who lived in those houses, and where had they learned to make that pottery? What were the people like in appearance? Ah, now the light is back again! But what has happened in between? What sudden storm visited this town, sweeping its houses into piles of debris and smashing its wares into thousands of pieces? Was the devastation wrought by raiders from the desert, or other riders from afar, who wiped out in a flash the wealth that labor and love had built up in centuries of civilized existence?

I have walked over the ruins of this ancient site, whose former name we do not know. Today it is called Khirbet Umm Hamad Sherqi, the "East Ruin of the Mother of Hamad." Fragments of pottery can be picked up in great numbers on the surface of an area

about a mile and a quarter long and a quarter of a mile wide (Fig. 70).
They are practically all that remain of a highly civilized center that
must have been widely known in its time. In fact, without the sherds,
it would be impossible to recognize the place as the location of an
ancient city. More pottery was once used there than exists in the
entire Jordan Valley today. The present inhabitants of the valley have
reverted to the use of skins for containers (Fig. 71). For them at
least, the art of ceramics is completely lost.

A thousand years went by before a new town sprang up about a
quarter of a mile west of the older site. After only a few hundred
years of existence it suffered the same fate of complete destruction.
It is the one now known as the "West Ruin of the Mother of
Hamad" (Khirbet Umm Hamad Gharbi). It is marked today by an
extensive, low rise, covered with pottery so typical of the period between approximately 2100 and 1900 B.C. (Middle Bronze I) that it
could be used as a classroom example of its kind. This area was apparently not again inhabited by sedentary agriculturists until the
Israelite period, during the Early Iron Age (thirteenth to the sixth
centuries B.C.). The two ruined sites are in the midst of fields now
once again being irrigated and cultivated. The present *fellahin*, who
live in tents, have already constructed mud-brick granaries, and, I am
confident, will soon build mud-brick villages to dwell in. Our day
may yet see the Jordan Valley dotted with thriving villages and towns
as of yore. And so scene succeeds scene upon the stage of history, as
the play goes on.

The rise and fall of Khirbet Umm Hamad Sherqi and Gharbi
illustrate a process that was to become heartbreakingly familiar in the
history of settlement in the Jordan Valley. Out of the era of earliest
antiquity appeared men striving blindly for better things. Small discoveries were chanced upon, experiences were passed on from father
to son, an ever increasing mass of knowledge was acquired. Civilization began, the land was tilled, and towns developed. Then such men
were replaced by others, less advanced and more rapacious. Ages of
emptiness set in, until pioneers again assembled to make new attempts on the same sites, or near them, because the physical factors

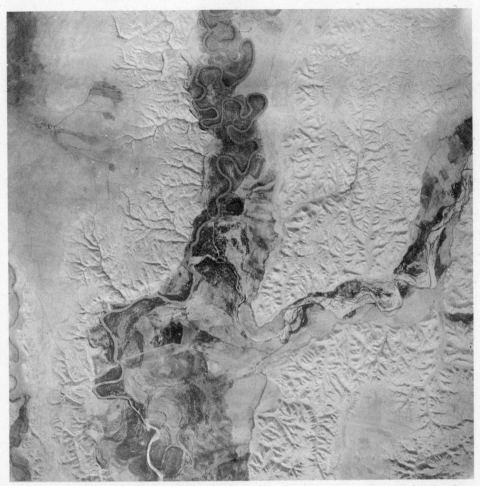

Photo by Royal Air Force, Levant

FIG. 72. The Jordan River snaking through its dark-green *Zor*, with the Jabbok emptying into it on the right, and part of the thin line of the Wadi Far'ah visible on the left. In the lower right center of the *Zor*, by its junction with the *Zor* of the Jabbok, is the small, white knoll of Tell Damieh (Biblical Adamah).

Fig. 73. Junction of the Jabbok (on the right) with the Jordan (on the left). Tell Damieh, the site of Biblical Adamah, is in the foreground.

FIG. 74. Tell Damieh (Biblical Adamah), in the Jordan Valley.

Fig., 75. Architectural reconstruction of Ezion-geber: Elath, as it appeared when rebuilt following the end of the Solomonic period. The gateway on the south side faces seaward.

left them no other choice. Thus a new civilization would be built up, and perhaps still further gains made, or perhaps it fell behind the one that had gone before. And after a while their effort would be eliminated by another invader, in the same manner as some careless creature might pull up an iris which had somehow sunk its roots and found nourishment in the desert. The history of the Jordan Valley is a history that conforms to its physical contours. It is a history of high peaks and low valleys, with desert areas in between. It is a history of achievement, ever annulled, ever renewed, with only one lasting gain to its credit, the recognition of the existence of the God of history.

The fourth millennium inhabitants of Khirbet Umm Hamad Sherqi did not belong to an isolated community in the Jordan Valley. On the contrary, they were part of a multitude that filled it in those days. I have found their traces on both sides of the Jordan, from the Lake of Galilee to Jericho, and from the Yarmuk River to the Dead Sea. Others before them had invented pottery, and already in the Neolithic period, during the sixth millennium B.C., had begun to irrigate, with all that that implies by way of a well-regulated, sedentary economy. Their presence is revealed by flints with the imprints of their handiwork, and by pottery made in a distinctive manner, not nearly so primitive as one might imagine from such an early age. Indeed the excellence of their attainments leaves the modern man frequently gasping with wonder.

6

Continuing southward, the sides of the narrowing plain crumble quickly down to the Jungle of the Jordan, which merges with the broadened banks of the Jabbok, as the two streams unite (Fig. 72). This area, irrigated by the Jabbok's waters, blooms into fragrant fertility, made all the more pleasant by contrast with the gaunt bareness of the hillsides above it. Dominating the rich bottom land is a small mound whose modern name, Tell Damieh, reflects the Biblical name of Adamah (Fig. 73). Its history began some time before the advent of the Israelites. The sherds found there show the coming and final disappearance of this people, and the arrival and departure of others after them down through the first centuries of the present era. The comparatively small tell, located on a natural rise (Fig. 74), guards the track to a crossing of the Jordan, whose position is approximately marked by the remains of a Roman bridge and by the new one which has now taken its place. Some years ago, a decrepit rope ferry plied its angular way across the swift current. Events alone, however, have scarred a mark at this point, which neither men nor time can easily efface.

The Israelites had passed through the desert, having survived its sands and vicissitudes. And then the longed-for day had come. Ahead of the people lay the Jordan, and across the Jordan lay the Promised Land! Priests, proudly burdened by the Ark of the Covenant and followed by the people, who were impatient to have done with this last obstacle to their final settlement, approached the flooded banks of the river, which for so long had been their sustaining dream. And just then, in that awful moment of uncertainty which marks the change from the rutted familiar to the uncertain new, an astounding miracle occurred. The Jordan was split in two! The river itself was an almost unbelievable miracle to these invaders from thirsty lands. To the wonder of its being was now added another wonder. As tradition has it, hardly had the feet of the priests touched the turbid flood, when "the waters coming from upstream stood still, forming a single solid mass, reaching [northward] from Adamah, as far as the fortress of Zarethan. And the waters going downstream to the Sea of the Arabah, the Salt Sea, were wholly cut off. . . . Whereupon the priests that carried the ark of the covenant of the Lord stood firmly on dry ground in the midst of the Jordan; and all Israel passed over on dry land, until the entire people had crossed over the Jordan" (Josh. 3:16, 17).

Is this a legendary portrayal of an incident which can be rationally explained? In this uneasy area of earthquakes, it is known that land slides have at times blocked the normal channel of the Jordan, forcing it to chart a new course. Did the Israelites chance upon just such an occasion, enabling them to cross the river dry-shod? Once before, according to the ancient account, during their escape from Egypt, they had passed between sundered walls of water of the Red Sea. Be that as it may, the first contact of Israel with the Jordan had in it the elements of a miracle, and the river remained strangely entwined with their subsequent history. From the very first it had fascinated them. To the very last it influenced their fortune and fate.

7

The wall of water, which, according to the Biblical description, stretched northward from Adamah to the Mezad, or Fortress, of Zarethan, bounded one of the richest sections of the east side of the Jordan Valley. One day, in that area, during the time when Solomon was building the Temple to the Lord in Jerusalem, a knot of workers was gathered around an earthen mold in a small foundry. They were silent. The air was still. Suddenly, a sigh of relief escaped them, and a glint of satisfaction lighted up momentarily the eyes of their leader. He was Hiram of Tyre, Solomon's master coppersmith. The copper pillars of Jachin and Boaz, which were to be set up at the porch of the Temple, had been successfully poured in their earthen molds. He had designed these pillars, and decorated them on the top with exquisite lily ornamentation. Now he could rest for a moment, relishing the satisfaction of work well done, before consigning it in his mind to the limbo of past accomplishment and tackling other tasks which stimulated anew his creative energies. Work was executed under his command at many places in the Jordan Valley. It was his duty and professional delight to provide for the Temple in Jerusalem sacred vessels and ornaments of metal, as shapely in form and exquisite in detail as could be found anywhere in his Phoenician homeland. "And king Solomon sent and fetched Hiram out of Tyre. He was the son of a widow of the tribe of Naphtali, and his father was a man of Tyre, a worker in copper. . . . And he came to king Solomon, and wrought all his work. . . . He set up [also] the pillars of the porch of the temple, calling the right pillar Jachin, and the left pillar Boaz. And upon the top of the pillars was lily-work" (I Kings 7:13, 21, 22). "All the vessels which Hiram made for king Solomon, in the temple of the Lord, were of burnished copper. In the plain [kikkar] of the

Jordan did the king have them cast, in thickened earthen molds, between Succoth and Zarethan" (I Kings 7:45, 46).

I have found fragments of slag on some of the tells north of Adamah and especially upon the site of ancient Succoth. In Solomon's time, this entire district in the Jordan Valley hummed with industrial activity devoted to the turning out of finished metal articles for the adornment of the new Temple. All day long, caravans of donkeys filed down into the valley from the eastern hills, bringing iron ore mined in the Ajlun area and charcoal from the forests of Gilead. Great slag heaps in the vicinity of modern Ajlun, north of the Jabbok, testify to the fact that some of the iron ore dug up near there was partly "roasted," before being transported down to the Jordan Valley for further refining.

Some raw materials were probably brought to Hiram's workshops from the Wadi Arabah, which, as we have seen, forms the southern part of the great fault in which also the Jordan Valley lies. The great copper and iron deposits which cover almost the entire length of the Wadi Arabah were operated at full blast in Solomon's time. Mining camps, slaves' quarters, small furnaces, and great slag heaps dot this desolate furrow all the way from the Dead Sea south to the Red Sea. How accurate were the words of Scripture which spoke of a "land whose stones are iron and out of whose hills you can dig copper" (Deut. 8:9)! And at Ezion-geber (Fig. 75), Solomon's seaport and industrial center at its south end, on the Gulf of Aqabah, the eastern arm of the Sinai-split Red Sea, we excavated a great refinery for metals. It is the largest and most complex of its kind ever recovered from antiquity. The ores already partly "roasted" at the mines in the Wadi Arabah were sent to Ezion-geber for further refinement. From that southernmost city of Solomon's power came ingots and finished metal articles for home consumption and for the foreign export trade.

This furious activity in the Wadi Arabah and at Ezion-geber was repeated on a smaller scale in the Jordan Valley. Plenty of water, close proximity to mines, accessibility to the then limitless wood supplies for charcoal, and nearness to Jerusalem made the region of

Succoth the center of widespread smelting and refining and manufacturing activities, without parallel there either before or after the time of Solomon. The master craftsman, Hiram of Tyre, had evidently approved of this part of the Jordan Valley as an area where he could make the most intricate castings. Clay for his molds abounded. What a scene must have greeted the eyes of the stranger who during this period visited the east side of the Jordan! Far and wide stretched rich fields of grain, carefully irrigated and continuously tended to see that each acre got its measure of water. In the middle of each large field stood the inevitable watchtower, where guards were mounted against the thieves by night. There too the laborers hied themselves at the noon rest hour, to eat their loaf of bread and drink their pitcher of water, and then, wrapping themselves up in their cloaks and looking like corpses in shrouds, sleep soundly, while the flies attacked them in vain. In the midst of these miles of cultivation were many villages, elevated on commanding heights. Clustered about some of the settlements were smelting furnaces and foundries, aflame with activity, directed by the superior skill of Solomon's Hiram of Tyre.

8

Outstanding among these cities was the site of Succoth (Fig. 76). It towered so commandingly above the plain in the Jordan Valley that it could be seen all the way from Adamah, some eight miles to the south of it. It is unquestionably to be identified with the outstanding ancient mound known today as Tell Deir'alla. How happy Jacob must have been to see it, after leaving Penuel on the Jabbok, where he had obtained a blessing from the Stranger who had wrestled with him during the night, and forgiveness from Esau, who had become reconciled with him the next day! Following the Jabbok downward, he and his people entered into the fair expanse of a very rich section of the Jordan Valley, which, in the Bible, is known as the *'emeq* (valley) of Succoth. In its midst stood the imposing mound, already ancient in Jacob's time. Here Jacob could rest from the ordeal he had been through at Penuel, and here his family could remain for a while, recovering from the hardships of the long journey from

Photo by Royal Air Force, Levant

FIG. 76. Tell Deir'alla (Succoth), a whitish mound in lower center of photograph, to left of upper bend of Wadi Zerqa (Jabbok). At extreme left, west of Tell Deir'alla, is Tell el-Ekhsas. At top left of photograph is Tell Mazar.

FIG. 77. The Mohammedan shrine of Nebi Musa (Prophet Moses), on the west side of the Jordan, with a view toward the Jericho plain.

149

Laban's lands far to the northeast. Here was forage for his flocks, land for plowing, water for all. Here he would call a long halt. "So Esau returned that day on his way unto Seir. And Jacob journeyed to Succoth, and built him a house, and made booths [*succoth*] for his cattle: therefore, the name of the place is called Succoth" (Gen. 33: 16, 17).

All this happened almost four thousand years ago. Jacob moved on to Palestine. Many centuries were to pass by before that country was invaded by the Philistines, coming from Mediterranean islands. In the struggle for the conquest of Canaan, the Israelites were finally to win out, but the Philistines were to bequeath it the name of Palestine. Meanwhile the centrally located and generally known Succoth continued to figure in history. Jacob's house and booths disintegrated into dust. Other and more permanent settlers built in his place after him, and they too vanished in time. A new city, still called Succoth, sprang up and flourished, as all cities in this irrigated valley flourished during any prolonged period of peace. Time passed. Gideon flashed by in pursuit of the raiders from Midian. The elders of Succoth, like those of Penuel, unluckily refused to give food to him and his men, who were faint from hunger. And when he returned that way, flushed with victory, he exacted severe revenge for their failure to help him in his hour of need. But the site of Succoth survived this visitation too. Soil and water kept some of the old settlers rooted, and attracted new ones.

Throughout the entire history of Israel, Succoth remained an important place. Solomon had his copper cast in earthen molds all the way from Succoth to Zarethan. The Bible speaks furthermore of Succoth and Zaphon, assuming that everybody had heard of them (Josh. 13:27). Finally, about the sixth century B.C. a blight of conquest and cumulative exhaustion hit Succoth, as it did its sister cities in the Jordan Valley. None of them ever really recovered. To be sure, during the subsequent Hellenistic, Roman, and Byzantine periods, small settlements established themselves successfully on the mound of Succoth. They, in turn, flourished and fell, receding into the forgetfulness of the past, which had also engulfed their predecessors.

Little more than fragments of pottery have remained to testify to their former existence.

Long before I got to Succoth (Tell Deir'alla), I could see it standing like a giant among its lesser fellows in the valley. What would this abandoned mass of houses and cities, risen high like a mighty anthill, be able to tell me? Which of its secrets could still be deciphered? Soon its steeply sloping sides loomed up in front of me. Around its base gurgled a stream, diverted from the Jabbok River to irrigate some neighboring fields. Climbing to the top of the mound, which rises about 60 feet above the level of the plain, I found it impossible to take a single step without treading on innumerable fragments of pottery. They were of all shapes and colors, ranging in time through many different civilizations. And as I collected samples of the sherds that littered the surface, it seemed to me that a veritable babel of sound burst out of the depths of the hill. The multitude of voices conveyed no clear meanings to me. I listened hard. Was that an Israelite expression, and the other a Midianite phrase? Were those Amorite accents and mingled with them the cadences of Canaanite speech? Did the deep gutturals belong to the still earlier dolmen builders, or to descendants of the prehistoric men who first peopled this valley? They all seemed to speak at once. Whose voices were those crying out of the ground, only to float away into a sea of silence? Today not a single soul lives on the tell. A few modern graves on the top mark the presence, in the vicinity, of some tent dwellers, who farm and irrigate a small part of the lands round about it and bury their dead on it.

I arranged the sherds I had gathered in separate piles, one group belonging to the time of the Israelites, another to the Late Bronze period that preceded them, and a third going back still earlier to the eighteenth to seventeenth centuries B.C. (Middle Bronze II b, c). "Look," I said to my companion, Rashid, "look at the beautiful burnished lines on this platter, which the ancient potter once proudly turned on his wheel. Look at the even bands of paint encircling this jar, with a band of white slip between them. Look, Rashid, and reflect that these specimens of pottery have outlasted by thousands of

years the men and women who made and used them. There were no
untilled lands here in ancient days, except when purposely left fallow.
Little water was wasted. Men lived in houses of thick mud-brick
walls, crowded within the fortifications. Yes, indeed they knew how
to read and write. On this very mound, perhaps on this particular
spot where we are now sitting, was the house of the boy whom Gideon seized on the outskirts of Succoth, and whom he compelled to
write down the names of the elders of the city, to their doom.

"Did they believe in God, do you ask, Rashid? Yes, they believed
in God. Before the time of the Israelites, the people who lived here
in the valley believed in many gods. When the Israelites arrived, they
brought with them the belief in one God. But only a handful of them
held firmly to this hard-won faith. Prophets and priests had constantly to enjoin the masses to worship God with good deeds and
not through offerings, with moral behavior and not through sweet-
smelling sacrifices or pious prayers emanating from a complacent
certainty that He was on their side. There were also many among
them who affirmed belief in the Lord but backslid to the pagan ob-
servances of Ashtoreth, trying to straddle two thresholds at one time.
As the centuries passed, however, they rejected all gods but God.
although they worshiped Him ever so imperfectly.

"Yes, Rashid, this God is the same as Allah. This is the God who
was worshiped by Moses and Joshua, but also by John the Baptist
and Jesus, and by Mohammed. He was worshiped here in Succoth,
here in the valley of the Jordan. Certainly, all of us can subscribe to
what you have just said: '*Allahu akbar*' (God is great, and there is
none beside him). But take no offense, Rashid, if we insist that Mohammed is only one of those who felt His presence more closely
than most ordinary mortals. No harm meant, Rashid, but was not
Jesus a prophet, and do you Mohammedans yourselves not speak of
Nebi Musa, the prophet Moses? Is it not so written in your own
Koran? Have you not, indeed, built a shrine to this Nebi Musa on
the west side of the Jordan (Fig. 77)? Let us say, '*El-hamdu lillah*'
(Praise be to God), in gratitude for being alive today, and praise him
whom also the makers of some of this ancient pottery worshiped.

Photo by Royal Air Force, Levant

FIG. 78. Tell el-Ekhsas (Mound of Booths) is seen in the upper right of the photograph above a salt depression in the cultivated *Ghor* part of the Jordan Valley, east of the *Zor* of the Jordan below it. It has wrongly been identified with Biblical Succoth.

FIG. 79. Looking west at Wadi Kufrinji, which crosses the east side of the Jordan Valley. Near its west end is Tell es-Saidiyeh (Biblical Zarethan). In the background, the *qattarah* hills bordering the *Zor* of the Jordan are visible, with the hills of Palestine rising above the west side of the *Ghor* level of the valley.

You and I, Rashid, through the religions that we profess, and through these fragments of pottery that we hold in our hands, link the past to the present. Men of Succoth, we, who are rooted in your past, salute your memory."

Succoth was not the only town in the 'emeq (valley) of Succoth. It had a number of smaller neighbors, all of them contemporary with it, and some of them with origins antedating it. Among them is the small mound of Tell el-Ekhsas, which is about a mile and a half west of it. Because of its modern Arabic name of Tell el-Ekhsas, which means the "Mound of Booths," it has been identified with the Biblical Succoth, which, as we have already seen, also means "Booths." Tell el-Ekhsas is situated in the center of the Jordan Valley, in the midst of fields still intricately irrigated. Its position is further marked by being above a very slight depression, a little more than a square mile in extent, which is too saline for agriculture (Fig. 78). There are no good archaeological reasons why this site should supersede Tell Deir'alla as being identified with Biblical Succoth. Its chief claim is the name "Mound of Booths," Tell el-Ekhsas. If this name reflects the ancient one of "Booths," Succoth, we must remember that it was not an uncommon practice for an ancient place name to shift from an abandoned site to a new one in the vicinity. These changes were particularly frequent in the Hellenistic-Roman period.

9

Two of the streams that flow across the east side of the Jordan Valley, cutting it, as if with a cleaver, into distinct sections, are the Wadi Rajeb and the Wadi Kufrinji. By each of these streams is located an extremely important tell. One of them is Tell Qos on the Wadi Rajeb. It is the site of the Biblical Zaphon, where Jephthah defeated the Ephraimites. The other, farther north, is the striking mound of Tell es-Saidiyeh (Fig. 79), near the western end of the Wadi Kufrinji. It is to be identified with the Biblical Zarethan. The height on which Zaphon was built marks the upper end of a rich district, whose lower limit is fixed by the towering tell of Succoth. From the hills just above them came the streams which conditioned their existence and prosperity. Comparable in importance to Zaphon and Succoth, but directly overlooking the Jordan at the western edge of this east side of the valley, were Adamah and Zarethan.

Zarethan is the site which figures in the Biblical account of the Israelites' crossing the Jordan on dry land, when the wall of water which dammed up the river reached "from Adamah as far as the fortress of Zarethan." It is mentioned too, as we have seen, in the description of Solomon's industrial activities in the Jordan Valley. "In the *kikkar* [plain], the king had them [copper vessels] cast, in the earthen foundries [or in the thickened earthen molds] between Succoth and Zarethan" (I Kings 7:46; II Chron. 4:17).

But how, on the basis of the two scanty references in the Bible mentioning Zarethan, can it be identified with any particular one of the numerous bleak, uninhabited, long-abandoned tells in the Jordan Valley? There are dozens of sites to choose from, dozens of nameless corpses of Biblical cities to confound speculation. In the verse which merely mentions the casting of copper vessels between Succoth and Zarethan, there is absolutely no hint as to where Zarethan might be, or even in what direction to look for it. However, a good deal of information can be squeezed out of the verse, which speaks of the wall of water reaching from Adamah as far as the fortress of Zarethan.

If it were necessary to try to convince a judge in court that the nameless waif of Tell es-Saidiyeh should have its legal name of Zarethan, and the historical heritage that goes with it, restored to it, we would list our reasons as follows:

(*a*) First of all, it is clear that Zarethan couldn't be south of Adamah, because the water downstream from Adamah stopped running, and had backed up as far north as Zarethan. Furthermore, there are no Biblical sites south of Adamah for a considerable distance. Nor would Zarethan be west of Adamah, because to say that the wall of water extended from the east to the west side of the river would not be saying anything. Naturally, it reached at least all the way to the western bank of the river, because otherwise the water would have continued to flow southward, and the crossing on dry land could not have been effected.

(*b*) All the verses that speak of the areas between Succoth and Zaphon, between Succoth and Zarethan, and between Adamah and Zarethan, refer to sites on the east side of the Jordan Valley, and list them from south to north.

(*c*) In view of the configuration of the Jordan Valley proper, which is about 125 feet above the *Zor*, or Jungle of the Jordan, through which the river flows, Zarethan would have to be close enough to the *Zor* of the Jordan to make it possible to say that the wall of water extended from Adamah to Zarethan. If Zarethan were situated in the center of the valley or near its eastern hills, neither the Jordan River nor its wider bed, the Jungle of the Jordan, could ever be seen from it.

(*d*) Zarethan would have to be situated by some source of water, preferably by the side of one of the streams that flow across the east side of the valley to empty finally into the Jordan.

(*e*) It seems obvious that Zarethan must have been a well-known landmark, the equivalent of a Dan or Beer-sheba elsewhere, because otherwise it would not have been mentioned in the Bible, which listed places only of obvious historical or topographical importance. In this connection, it must have been so important a settlement that when a Jerusalemite, for instance, heard of it, he could say to himself, "Yes, I know where it is."

(*f*) It is likely that a place like Zarethan would have been occupied not only in the time of the Israelites, when the Bible was written, but also much earlier, when the same physical factors making for its importance were present.

(*g*) And finally, the pottery found on the logical site would have to conform to the periods in history when it is known to have been occupied, to judge from such evidence as is contained in the Bible or in other ancient records.

The actual archaeological facts agree completely with the conclusions to be derived from a careful examination of Josh. 3:16. This verse was meant to be taken literally, to the effect that the Jordan River was dammed up from Adamah as far as Zarethan, enabling the Israelites freely and easily to cross on dry land to the west side of the

Jordan. There is only one place in the entire Jordan Valley that meets the above specifications, and that is the site of Tell es-Saidiyeh.

Tell es-Saidiyeh is situated about 12 miles north-northeast of Adamah. It is on the east side of the river, being only about a mile from it on top of the edge of the *Ghor* part of the valley, which overlooks the Jordan and its *Zor*, or Jungle. Immediately below the north side of Tell es-Saidiyeh is the Wadi Kufrinji, which empties into the Jordan (Fig. 79). And it is just at this point, below the north side of the long, high mound, that numerous fine springs appear, further to swell the volume of the stream of the Wadi Kufrinji. Beyond the east side of the tell stretches a wide and fertile reach of the Jordan Valley. The waters of the Wadi Kufrinji are partly used to irrigate some of the rich adjacent lands. It cuts a clear, though shallow, path for itself on its way across the valley to the Jordan, and serves as a boundary line between the areas to the north and south of it.

There are other ancient sites along the Wadi Kufrinji, east of Tell es-Saidiyeh, but none is of large importance. Tell es-Saidiyeh is the outstanding mound in this entire section of the valley. From the hills to the east it can be seen looming up in the distance like a strong citadel—which, indeed, is just what it was. The mound guards the approach to western Palestine, and bars the way to the rich valley east of it. People in the hill country on both sides of the Jordan could not but have known of it. And the large quantities of sherds found on it show not only that it was densely inhabited in Israelite times, but that it had been occupied as early as the Chalcolithic period. No place in the Jordan Valley meets the requirements for identification with Zarethan as well as Tell es-Saidiyeh does.

There is striking confirmation of this conclusion. In the third century A.D., there lived a learned man in Palestine who described the relative positions of Adamah and Zarethan as being 12 miles distant from each other. He was Rabbi Johanan, whose words are recorded in the Talmud, which is full of important topographical allusions. He could easily have known the actual site of Zarethan, whose Biblical name had apparently not yet been forgotten in his day, more than a millennium and a half ago.

VI

Mountain Streams and Valley Cities:
The Upper Basin

I

NORTH of the Wadi Kufrinji is the Wadi Yabis, whose stream races through a deep canyon before it reaches the level of the Jordan Valley. With blessed tenacity, it has clung in modern form to its ancient name, which must have been the River Jabesh. "Jabesh" has a familiar ring to our ears. Does not the Bible speak frequently of Jabesh-gilead, the famous city on the east side of the Jordan Valley? Had not cruel punishment once been meted out to its residents for failing to join in the expedition against the tribe of Benjamin, some of whose members had mishandled the Levite's concubine? The town was put to the sword, only four hundred virgins being saved. Through some strange quirk of tribal justice, they were thereupon given to the decimated tribe of Benjamin to replenish its numbers (Judg. 21:8–14). And, on another occasion, had not the men of Jabesh-gilead been saved through the intervention of Saul from having their right eyes put out by Nahash the Ammonite as a lasting "reproach upon all Israel" (I Sam. 11:1–13)? This demonstration on Saul's part of a far-reaching responsibility for fellow Israelites was a kindness which the men of Jabesh-gilead were not soon to forget.

Saul's star, and Israel's fortunes with it, rose fast, but fell even more suddenly. The long-drawn-out struggle between Israel and the invaders from the sea resulted in a temporary victory for the Philistines at the Battle of Gilboa near Beth-shan. "And the battle went sore against Saul, and the archers overtook him. . . . Then said Saul to his armorbearer, Draw thy sword, and thrust me through, lest these uncircumcised come and do it, and abuse me. But his armorbearer would not; for he was sore afraid. Therefore Saul took his sword, and fell upon it. Whereupon . . . his armorbearer . . . too fell upon his sword, and died with him. So Saul died, and his three sons, and his armorbearer, and all his men, the same day together. . . . And it came to pass on the morrow, when the Philistines came to strip the slain, that they found Saul and his three sons fallen on mount Gilboa. And they cut off his head, and stripped off his armor. . . . And they put his armor in the temple of Ashtaroth; and they fastened his body to the wall of Beth-shan" (ch. 31:3-10).

News travels fast in the almost self-contained Jordan Valley. Wherever we camped in its upper reaches, even as far south as Succoth, on the River Jabbok, we knew practically within the day what had transpired at Beisan. Travelers from one encampment to another relayed constant reports from it. And so it was in ancient times, only more so, because there were more people and more activity then in the Jordan Valley than there are now. Certainly within a few hours after Saul's body had been shamefully impaled on the city wall of Beth-shan, news of the indignity had spread far and wide in the valley. And no village there was more vitally concerned with what had happened to Saul than Jabesh-gilead, which was located southeast of Beth-shan on the east side of the Jordan.

One of the Jabeshites had probably been in Beth-shan during the morning, witnessed the degrading spectacle, and writhed at the Philistine glee. That very afternoon he returned home and related how he had seen the corpses of the princes of Israel staked out like slain animals. The elders tore their cloaks and capped their heads with dust. The entire population made loud lament. Was there nothing to be done? "Men of Jabesh-gilead," said one of their leaders, "can we allow the bodies of our brothers to rot under another day's sun, further to be feasted upon by vultures and to be stoned and spit at by these Philistine dogs—may God blot out their memory!" All agreed instantly that it was their obvious duty somehow or other to rescue the corpses and give them honorable burial.

Darkness fell. Chosen groups of men sallied forth from Jabesh-gilead, moved northward, forded the Jordan, and climbed the broad benches of land which rose like great steps up to the Plain of Beth-shan. They knew every track that led up to the great citadel, and every narrow, twisting alley inside it. Somehow they gained access to the city, where they had relatives and friends. Perhaps the Philistines, flushed with victory, were not keeping careful watch that night. Stealthily the Jabeshites slipped through the shadows, and clambered up to and over the battlements. Silently, speedily, they cut loose the bodies of their benefactors, and lowered them to some of their companions waiting below. They wrapped them in shrouds brought for the purpose. Now for the journey homeward! Willing hands carried the heavy burdens in changing shifts. They recrossed the Jordan, climbed up from the Jungle to the level of the valley proper, and some hours later were back at Jabesh-gilead. Having left just after dark, they had returned before dawn. The gates of the fortress on top of its high hill were swung open to receive them, after they had purified themselves. The bodies were left outside and burned clean of the defilement they had suffered. After that, the bones were wrapped in the finest raiment available, and then, to the accompaniment of the singing of sad psalms, interred under a sacred tree in the near-by cemetery. The men of Jabesh-gilead had acquitted themselves honorably. To the best of their ability, they had repaid the debt they owed the noble dead, who while living had once saved them from shame worse than death.

"And when the inhabitants of Jabesh-gilead heard . . . what the Philistines had done to Saul, all the valiant men arose, and marched all night, and took the body of Saul and the bodies of his sons from the wall of Beth-shan; and they returned to Jabesh [that very same night], and burnt them there. And they took their bones, and buried them under the tamarisk-tree in Jabesh. After that, they fasted seven days" (vs. 11–13).

Later on, when David was anointed king in Saul's place, he sent a special message to the inhabitants of Jabesh-gilead, promising to hold them in good regard for this act of faithfulness to Saul. "And David sent messengers unto the men of Jabesh-gilead, and said unto them, Blessed be ye of the Lord, that ye have showed this kindness unto your lord, even unto Saul, and have buried him. . . . And I also will requite you this kindness" (II Sam. 2:5, 6). The tamarisk tree of Jabesh has, of course, long since disappeared, but the ancient site itself and the memory of the mercy of its citizens still endure. It is appropriate, though not significant, that the part of Jabesh-gilead where perhaps the remains of Saul and his sons were buried should today be called "Meqbereh," that is, "a burial place." There is not, however, a single ancient site in the entire Jordan Valley that has not been seized upon by modern Arabs to bury their dead.

Late one afternoon, Rashid Hamid and I rode up to the tents of the Zeinati Arabs, pitched near the point where the Wadi Yabis enters the Jordan Valley. For generations explorers had sought the site of Jabesh-gilead, looking for it, correctly enough, along the Wadi Yabis, the River Jabesh. Should we be any more successful? Tribesmen ran out, seized the reins, and begged us to dismount. In Mohammed Zeinati's absence, his youngest brother, who was present, came forward to meet us and to lead us to the places of honor in the great guest tent, near the fireplace. The coals were blown on to start a fresh flame, and more fuel was added. Already one of the slaves had roasted coffee beans and was pounding them in the urn with rhythmical beat. He was preparing the bitter brew that the Arab host invariably offers his guest, and himself sips at intervals all day long. Then sweet tea was served, together with a light snack in anticipation of the *dhabiheh*, the sheep slaughtered the moment after we came, which would be served to us later in the evening.

As soon as decorum permitted after our arrival, and before the benumbing evening meal had to be attacked, I directed the conversation to the subject of *khirab*, "ruins." The assembled company assured us that there was nothing in the region that would interest us, thinking we should be attracted only by great above-surface ruins, standing pillars, and the like. It was hard to make them understand that any little mound with fragments of pottery on it came within our concern. I felt certain that somewhere in the immediate vicinity of the encampment itself, with the fine stream of the Wadi Yabis issuing forth from the near-by hills to make possible the irrigation of thousands of fine acres of rich valley land, there were bound to be found ancient Biblical and pre-Biblical sites. Hereabouts should be the site of Jabesh-gilead itself! One could almost figure out and mark on a map the theoretical position of Jabesh-gilead on the east side of the Jordan Valley, merely by a careful perusal and checking of the Biblical accounts dealing with this place.

When Saul's army relieved Jabesh-gilead from the siege by Nahash the Ammonite, it marched first to Bezek, at the edge of the hills overlooking the Jordan Valley from the west. Descending at night into the valley and fording the Jordan it reached Jabesh-gilead in the early watch of the morning, made a surprise attack upon the unsuspecting Ammonites, and utterly defeated them. This story, which there is no reason to disbelieve, clearly indicates that Jabesh-gilead was on the east side of the Jordan Valley, so near to the point of departure at Bezek that the march and surprise attack could be made under the cover of darkness in the course of one night. It can be assumed that Jabesh-gilead would be located by some source of water, and in this instance certainly alongside of the Wadi Yabis. The area to be examined is considerably lessened by this consideration. Had Jabesh-gilead been situated farther east, where it has previously been thought to be, in the hills above the valley, Saul's strategy would have had to be completely different. He could not then have reached his goal in one night's march, nor have attacked under cover of darkness. By the same token, if Jabesh-gilead were located somewhere in the eastern hills, even though overlooking the Wadi Yabis, it would have been impossible for the men of Jabesh-gilead to receive on the same day the news of the infamy perpetrated on the bodies of Saul and his sons, and that same night to steal to Beth-shan, retrieve the bodies, and bring them back to Jabesh-gilead for burial. Clearly, then, Jabesh-gilead had to be in the valley proper, on the east side of the Jordan, by the Wadi Yabis, and within a comparatively few miles of Beth-shan.

All these things ran through my mind again, as I sat in the tent of Mohammed Zeinati and sipped coffee served by his chief black slave, Abd Ihmeid Abdul-Heir. It was about an hour before nightfall when we went out to walk up and down in front of the tent and "breathe the air." About half a mile to the east I espied a low, insignificant-looking mound, which might have been natural, but which again resembled the low knolls, slightly lighter in color than their surroundings, that experience had taught me to recognize as ancient sites. I asked my companions whether or not it had a name. "*Billah* [by Allah]," they replied, "it is called *Tell el-Meqbereh.*" "*Tell el-Meqbereh?*" I echoed in pleased surprise. "The Tell of the Burial Place?" Sometimes, to be sure, a place may be called a "tell," and not be an antiquity site at all, as, for instance, Tell Sleihat, south of Tell el-Meqbereh. Tell Sleihat is a high, completely isolated, imposing-looking hill, which has the typical flattish top and sloping sides that are characteristic of many artificial tells. It is, however, a completely natural hill, as I can testify from a meticulous examination, repeated on several occasions. Normally, however, if a place is called a tell, there is every reason to assume that it is an artificial city-hill, formed by successive towns each built on the ruins of the preceding one.

It was all that I could do to refrain from rushing over immediately to Tell el-Meqbereh and commencing to search for the fragments of pottery which reveal the ages of occupation on a site as clearly as tree rings disclose the age and life history of a tree. As soon as possible, early the next morning, we rode over to the site. Our most sanguine hopes were fulfilled. Large quantities of sherds of all kinds were found, many of them belonging to Israelite times from about the thirteenth to the sixth centuries B.C., with others going as far back, approximately, as 3200 B.C., that is, to the beginning of the Early Bronze Age.

It was like springtime in the Jordan Valley when we first visited Tell el-Meqbereh in December, 1942. The fields round about the low mound were lush green with growths of all kinds. Flocks of sheep and goats, and herds of cattle, belonging to the well-to-do Zeinati Arabs, grazed there all day long. Part of the lands near by were being plowed for the spring planting. Oxen and camels were pulling pointed sticks of plows across the fields, and it could have been an inhabitant of Jabesh-gilead who was supervising the entire activity,

FIG. 80. The twin sites of Tell el-Meqbereh (in foreground) and Tell Abu Kharaz on hilltop behind it, which are to be identified with ancient Jabesh-gilead.

165

instead of one of the relatives of Mohammed Zeinati. The planted
fields would be irrigated at the proper time by the waters of the Wadi
Yabis, which flowed almost immediately below the south side of the
mound. The pastoral scene, with its Biblical aspect, lent lifelike
quality to the slumbering site of Tell el-Meqbereh.

Several hundred yards east of Tell el-Meqbereh a high flat-topped
hill stands alone, like an advance sentinel of the slopes which mount
steeply to the broken plateau of northern Gilead. The unfriendly
sides of this hill, cultivated only at the very bottom, soon rise abruptly
for some distance, revealing great ribs of rock, stripped naked of all
covering of soil. A mean track leads up to its top, which we found
had once been completely surrounded by a great stone wall. Large
sections of this outer fortification could still be traced. Despite a lux-
uriant growth of weeds, a considerable quantity of sherds was found,
duplicating those picked up at Tell el-Meqbereh. Indeed, we had
first been led to the examination of this isolated hill by reason of a
broad trail of fragments of pottery which seemed to connect it with
Tell el-Meqbereh. Questioning revealed then that the anciently occupied hilltop was called Tell Abu Kharaz. It completely dominates
the Wadi Yabis, after it leaves its deep gorge in the eastern hills and
moves westward across the valley to the Jordan. There is a fine view
from Tell Abu Kharaz as far as Beisan and Tell el-Husn, the mound
of ancient Beth-shan, and the distance between them can be walked
in a few hours. Actually, Tell Abu Kharaz and Tell el-Meqbereh
must be considered as one site, the latter being the residential section
of the great fortress towering directly above it. This double site is the
only one which agrees with all the Biblical data concerning Jabesh-
gilead (Fig. 80).

That night we stayed in the tent of Aref Zeinati, his elder brother
Mohammed having moved his camp some distance away. Zeinati's
tent was pitched in the Jordan Valley, close to the Wadi Yabis, and
directly across from the hill surmounted by the ruins of the ancient
fortress of Jabesh-gilead. I told the story of its past to the assembled
Arabs who sat around the fireplace in the tent, and in whose veins
some of the blood of the men of Jabesh-gilead may still flow. They

cultivate the same lands. They lead much the same lives. The interest of my listeners was so keen, their questions so to the point, that soon I almost forgot to whom I was talking. Were these the Arabs of Zeinati, or were these the Israelites of Jabesh-gilead? It was all I could do to refrain from turning to one of them and asking him how it was on that memorable night that the men of Jabesh-gilead had got past the Philistine guards on the city wall of Beth-shan! Or had none been posted that evening? To an archaeologist who can, so to speak, quicken the artifacts of bygone civilizations with the breath of life, there is frequently no perceptible difference between what was and is. Events and people and places, not of days or years, but of centuries and millenniums, have a tendency to telescope themselves in his thinking.

2

From Jabesh-gilead we followed the Wadi Yabis (River Jabesh) upstream eastward into the hills of Gilead. Very soon, however, we were forced to abandon its direct course, as its canyon walls gained in steepness. Descending from the broken plateau, we came to a bend in the stream, where, during the ages, it had cut down the hills to make room for a little valley, which was carefully cultivated and irrigated. Grain grows richly there, and small groves of lemon and fig trees flourish, yielding much fruit in season. Directly overlooking this hidden garden area is a large hill, called Tell el-Maqlub. On it are the remains of an extensive ancient site. The hill is cultivated from bottom to top in roughly terraced benches, planted largely to grain. There are some vineyards in the vicinity. Around the top of the hill can be seen clear vestiges of a strong outer wall, which enclosed the settlements once located there. Further traces of extensive occupation were furnished by large quantities of pottery fragments strewn over the top and sides of the hill. This pottery was mainly of Israelite origin or earlier.

Tell el-Maqlub has sometimes previously been identified with Jabesh-gilead, not because of its pottery, for which earlier explorers never looked, but merely because it was located by the Wadi Yabis.

They were not aware of the existence of the great double site of Tell Abu Kharaz and Tell el-Meqbereh, which escaped attention. Nor did they consider that news from the Jordan Valley penetrates but slowly and accidentally into the highlands of Gilead and their isolated villages, of which Tell el-Maqlub was one. Its residents might not have learned for days what had transpired at Beth-shan. The hillsmen now dwelling near Tell el-Maqlub know practically nothing of what goes on at Beisan today. The seminomadic Arabs, however, who live in the northern part of the Jordan Valley, know within a few hours what happens there. In addition, from Tell el-Maqlub to Beisan is a good six or seven hours' walk each way. The men of Tell el-Maqlub could scarcely have reached Beth-shan and returned, carrying the bodies of Saul and his sons, in the course of one night.

If, however, Tell el-Maqlub is definitely not to be identified with Jabesh-gilead, there is much reason for identifying it with Abel-meholah. The name Abel-meholah wandered in the abbreviated form of Abel, during the Hellenistic period, to a near-by site marked today by an Arab village, which is still known as Kefr Abil. In the case of another Biblical site, located in the lower Jordan Valley, when the location was shifted the name was changed from Abel-Shittim to Abila, the equivalent of Abel. The main historical importance of Abel-meholah lies in the fact that it was the home of Elisha the Prophet. Like Elijah, he too was a native of Transjordan. Hitherto, however, the site of Abel-meholah has been located by everybody on the west side of the Jordan, largely because of a completely erroneous identification made by the geographer Eusebius (A.D. 260–340). He identified it with Bethmaela, ten (Roman) miles south of Scythopolis (Beth-shan), on the basis, apparently, of vague similarity of names.

Everything points to the fact that Abel-meholah was a hill city and not a lowland town. It would have been much more to the point had attention been paid to the simple sense of Abel-meholah, which means the "Vale of Dancing," than to make impossible philological comparisons. One is reminded of the Benjaminites, who hid in the vineyards at Shiloh and seized the maidens for wives when they came out to dance the dances (*meholah*) of the grape festival (Judg. 21:

20, 21). And one recalls furthermore the defeat which Jephthah inflicted upon the Ammonites, smiting them from Aroer as far as Abel-
keramim, the "Vale of Vineyards." These places were situated by
running streams of water and in hilly country devoted to the culture
of the grapevine. There are numerous similar areas in Transjordan
today, such as around Salt, Na'ur, Sweileh, and Suf, where grapes
have been grown for thousands of years. The name of Abel-meholah,
the "Vale of Dancing," probably originated from the hilly grape
country where it was situated, and where at harvesttime the grape
festival was celebrated with joyous dances. Tell el-Maqlub is ideally
situated for the location of Abel-meholah. And it would have been at
Tell el-Maqlub (Abel-meholah) that Elijah stopped on his way north,
from Horeb in Sinai to Damascus in Syria, to see Elisha.

3

Elijah had fled to the sacred mountain in Sinai to escape the wrath
of Ahab's wife, the Phoenician princess Jezebel. He had been instru-
mental in confounding and destroying at Mount Carmel the prophets
of her god, Baal. At Sinai, Elijah had been enjoined to depart on a
threefold mission: to travel to Damascus, where he was to help to
crown Hazael as king of Syria; in his own country to anoint Jehu as
king of Israel; and finally, to consecrate Elisha as his successor. He
was able to accomplish only the last of these tasks, it being left to
Elisha to complete the first two (II Kings 8:7–15; 9:1–13). The very
undertaking by Elijah of this journey spelled the coming of age of
Israelite prophecy. It was henceforth in increasing measure to stress
that all affairs of men were the concern of God. And the true prophet
was to function, not as an onlooker, and even less as a professional
soothsayer, but as an agent of God's moral order. Neither war nor
politics nor private affairs were to be outside the scope of prophetic
concern. The man of God was to speak the Word of God regardless
of consequence to himself, zealous only to obey the categorical im-
perative of divine law and revelation.

The road to the homes of Elisha and Hazael led through Transjordan in a straight line, practically, from one to another. Jehu was

finally anointed king at Ramoth-gilead, which we have identified
with Tell Ramith in northern Transjordan, near the Syrian border.
The first stage of his journey led Elijah to his native haunts, where
Elisha too was at home. After all, was not Elijah a native of Jabesh-
gilead, a few miles below Abel-meholah in the Jordan Valley? A
small scribal error has crept into the Biblical text, causing much confusion with regard to Elijah's birthplace, although it has always been
abundantly clear that he came from the east side of the Jordan. He is
described in I Kings 17:1 as "Elijah the Tishbite, of the *toshabē*
Gilead," which is usually translated as "Elijah the Tishbite, of the
sojourners of Gilead." That is vague to the point of exasperation.
The correct reading, which restores Elijah to his proper background,
should probably be: "Elijah the Jabeshite, from Jabesh-gilead."

And in this connection, it is perhaps now possible to clear up another mystery with which the account of the life of Elijah has long
been burdened, namely, the location of the famous Brook Cherith.
Here again there has been much confusion, because scholars as well
as novelists have not paid sufficient attention to the literal meaning
of the Biblical text. Continuing the story which commences with the
mention of "Elijah the Jabeshite, of Jabesh-gilead," the Biblical
narrative reads: "And the word of the Lord came unto him (Elijah),
saying, Get thee hence, and turn thee *eastward*, and hide thyself by
the brook Cherith, before [east of] the Jordan. And it shall be, that
thou shalt drink of the brook; and I have commanded the ravens to
feed thee there. So he went and did according to the word of the
Lord, dwelling by the brook Cherith, before [east of] the Jordan.
And the ravens brought him bread and flesh in the morning, and
bread and flesh in the evening; and he drank of the brook. And it
came to pass after a while, that the brook dried up, because there was
no rain in the land" (I Kings 17:2–7). It is explicitly stated in the
text that when Elijah went to hide himself by the side of the Brook
Cherith he went eastward (in Transjordan toward the desert).

The prophets turned ever to the stern simplicity of the desert.
They sought to perpetuate the clear-cut standards of brotherhood
and belief in God which had first come into the consciousness of

FIG. 81. A shepherd watering his flock at a rain-filled depression in the desert in eastern Transjordan.

Israel during its desert days. Twice in his lifetime Elijah sought refuge in the desert, first of Transjordan, and then of Sinai. In later centuries Paul of Tarsus was to turn to the eastern desert to renew his strength. For three years he stayed in the desert before re-entering the arena of the world at Damascus.

The Brook Cherith was undoubtedly a small wadi, usually with some water in it, but drying up on occasion. It may well have been one of the easternmost branches of the River Jabesh, whose roots extend into the very desert. There Elijah hid himself from the wrath of Ahab of Israel. Afraid of nought save the God he served, Elijah had promised Ahab that divine punishment would be visited upon him for his waywardness in worshiping Baal and Ashtoreth in his capital city of Samaria. He foretold a famine in the land of Israel: "As the Lord, the God of Israel, liveth, before whom I stand, there shall not be dew nor rain these years, but according to my word" (v. 1). Elijah fled then to the Brook Cherith, near the desert east of his home at Jabesh-gilead. As a youth he had probably shepherded flocks there in the springtime after the early rains (Fig. 81).

It cannot, however, be proved that the Brook Cherith is in or near the eastern beginnings of the River Jabesh. One thing, nevertheless, is beyond debate. The Brook Cherith is emphatically not to be identified, as for instance by George Moore in his magnificent novel *The Brook Kerith*, with the Wadi Qelt, which runs from below Jerusalem to Jericho, and then across the west side of the valley to the Jordan. The Brook Cherith is just as certainly on the east side of the Jordan as are Abel-meholah and Jabesh-gilead.

Elijah's way to Abel-meholah to find Elisha was an easy one for him. He could almost have gone there blindfolded from Jabesh-gilead, which he would probably have visited first, en route from the valley to the hills of Gilead. I have said that Elijah's way was easy for him. And so it must have been for one who had spent his childhood and youth along the reaches of the River Jabesh, knowing exactly where the best grazing lay for his father's flocks, and at what times of the year to lead them there, and when to turn them toward the stream to drink their fill. But from another point of view this was the most difficult journey that Elijah had ever undertaken in his life. Nearing the end of his career, he was about to lay the mantle of successorship upon his disciple Elisha. The future belonged to his pupil. His own day was almost over, and the time for his departure from this world had arrived.

"So he [Elijah] departed thence, and found Elisha the son of Shaphat, who was plowing, with twelve yoke of oxen before him, and he with the twelfth: and Elijah passed over unto him, and cast his mantle upon him. Whereupon he left the oxen, and ran after Elijah, and said unto him, Let me, I pray thee, kiss my father and my mother, and then I will follow thee. And he replied to him, Go back again; for what have I done unto thee? And he returned from following him, and took the yoke of oxen, and slew them, and boiled their flesh with the instruments of the oxen, and gave unto the people, and they did eat. Then he arose, and went after Elijah, and ministered unto him" (ch. 19:19–21). When I visited Tell el-Maqlub, the *fellahin* were engaged in plowing on both sides of the adjacent perennial stream of the Wadi Yabis (River Jabesh), with just about a dozen yoke of oxen all told. A simple Arab peasant halted his team of oxen to greet me, and to answer my questions about the countryside. Was there any connection, however tenuous, between him and that other peasant, who long centuries before had been plowing in his place?

The last act in the life of Elijah was yet to take place. And where else but along the east side of the Jordan, where his life had begun? From Gilgal on the Jordan to Beth-el in the hills near Jerusalem, and again from Beth-el past Ai down to Jericho in the valley below, Elijah traced a pilgrim's circle, accompanied by his disciple, Elisha, whom he could not persuade to leave his side. "Elijah the Jabeshite is here," was the common cry as soon as he was seen. Who did not know by sight or reputation "the hairy man girt with a girdle of leather about his loins" (II Kings 1:8)? And who was not aware that this would be his last visit, and that this was a last leave-taking? Finally the two men stood again by the Jordan, and they crossed over to the east bank. There the pupil prayed for a double portion of his master's spirit, and he received the blessing for which he asked.

In what vivid terms is described the departure of Elijah from the world of laborious effort to the heavenly sphere of miraculous happenings! "And they two [Elijah and Elisha] stood by the Jordan. And Elijah took his mantle, and wrapped it together, and smote the waters, and they were divided . . . , so that they two went over on dry ground. And it came to pass, when they were gone over, that Elijah said unto Elisha, Ask what I shall do for thee, before I am taken from thee. And Elisha said, I pray thee, let a double portion of thy spirit be upon me. And he said, Thou hast asked a hard thing: however, if thou see me when I am taken from thee, it shall be so unto thee; but if not, it shall not be so. And it came to pass, . . . that there appeared a chariot of fire, and horses of fire, which parted them both asunder; and Elijah went up by a whirlwind unto heaven. And Elisha saw it, and he cried, My father, my father, the chariots of Israel and the horsemen thereof!" (ch. 2:7–12).

Elisha thereupon assumed the burden of prophecy, recrossing the Jordan, and carrying on in the footsteps of his master. "And when he [Elisha] saw him no more, he took hold of his own clothes, and rent them into two pieces. He took up also the mantle of Elijah, and went back, and stood by the bank of the Jordan, . . . and smote the waters, and said, Where is the Lord, the God of Elijah? and when he also had smitten the waters, they were divided . . .; and Elisha went over. And when the followers of the prophets that were at Jericho over against him saw him, they said, The spirit of Elijah doth rest on Elisha. And they came to meet him, and bowed themselves to the ground before him" (vs. 12–15). Such, however, on occasion, is the lack of honor for a prophet in his own country that when Elisha left Jericho, and started climbing the hills back to Beth-el, some "young lads came out of the city and mocked, and said unto him, Go up, thou baldhead; go up, thou baldhead" (v. 23). But, sad to relate, the children were thereupon devoured by bears (v. 24).

4

Occasionally one finds references to ancient Jordan Valley villages in records which are much earlier than the time of Elijah and older than the Bible, and which substantiate the evidence of pottery remains. Such records exist in the form of Egyptian name lists and cuneiform tablets. Most of the latter have hitherto been found in Egypt, but they were written in Babylonian by Palestinian rulers to their Egyptian overlord. These records date mainly from the fourteenth century B.C. In one of these el-Amarna tablets is a message from a Canaanite princess, with the resounding name of Lady-of-the-Lions, written apparently to Amenophis IV. In it the place of her residence is mentioned as being at Sapuna, which is the equivalent of the Biblical Zaphon (Tell Qos).

In another of the el-Amarna letters, mention is made of Pihilu, which was later to become known as Pella, and is now called Tabaqat Fahil. Crossing the swiftly flowing Wadi Jurm at the point of its entrance into the valley, one gazes upward to the great fortress mound of Tabaqat Fahil (Pella), situated high up in the hills, like an eagle's nest on a ledge, hard to reach from either above or below. It occupies a unique position with regard to the Jordan Valley, being neither part of it nor completely separated from it. A track winds past Pella, once good enough to carry chariot traffic and donkey trains. In the Roman period it helped to connect Pella with its confederated cities of the Decapolis, of which it was an outstanding member. The steep slopes above Pella lead down, at the east end of the shelf on which it is situated, into a caldronlike hollow. Along its sides there gushes forth a whole series of springs, sweet and clear, and so strong that within a few hundred yards a rushing stream is formed, which plunges headlong down to the floor of the valley. It was inevitable that men should settle by this gathering of waters, and build houses and temples and strong fortifications.

From the huge guest tent of the patriarchal Emir Ya'qub Hamzeh, pitched in the valley near Jisr Sheikh Hussein, a walk of several hours brought us to Tabaqat Fahil. There we were met and entertained at lunch by Dhiab Suleiman, the *mukhtar* ("headman") of the village. It mattered not that he was poorly clothed, his house small, his people poverty-stricken. It mattered not that the members of his small community squatted like gypsies among massive ruins, whose humblest dwelling must have been a mansion compared to any of theirs. We were exchanging polite conversational amenities with a prince of Pella. We drank his coffee, which slaked our thirst. We dipped pieces of his fragrant, freshly baked bread into a dish of sour milk, and ate the eggs which he boiled and peeled for us. We exclaimed honestly over the goodness of it all. Inwardly we hoped that his family would not go hungry that day because of this drain on their slender store of supplies. We could under no circumstances have refused his hospitality or stoned him with disdain or pity for his slender provender. I have forgotten many splendid feasts, but I shall never forget the bread we broke with him. The invitation to his board was a royal summons, and we commoners had no choice but to obey. I photographed him, his hand resting on a fragment of a fine Corinthian capital, with which his children had been playing in the courtyard. Then he guided us about the ruins, and we explained to him the significance of some of them: Roman bastions, Byzantine church foundations, medieval glazed Arabic pottery. He exclaimed over the age of the sherds, belonging, as we told him, variously to Arabs and Byzantines, to Romans and Israelites, and to others still earlier.

Photo by American Schools of Oriental Research

FIG. 82. Fragments of 4th millennium B.C. painted "band-slip" pottery from Tell edh-Dhiabeh
on the west side of the Jordan Valley.

Photo by S. J. Schweig, Jerusalem

FIG. 83. Tell el-Husn, the site of ancient Beth-shan: Scythopolis, with modern Beisan visible beyond it.

VII

Path of Pilgrims

I

THE west side of the Jordan Valley is narrower and much less watered by perennial streams than the east side, being neither so full of settlements nor mentioned so frequently in the Bible. No two and a half tribes, requiring special consideration, were separating themselves on that side from the rest of Israel. But there too, wherever water was to be had with which to irrigate land, men gathered together in sedentary communities, tilling the soil from early prehistoric times onward. To cross over into it had required a long struggle. Joshua and his namesake, Jesus, left their imprint on its history. It has long been the path of pilgrims. Several of its cities achieved outstanding importance and lasting fame. Most of its inhabited places, like those on the east side, remained nameless in the Bible. The names of a few of them were preserved only in earlier records, as that of Rehob, mentioned, for instance, in an Egyptian stele of the fourteenth century B.C. found at Beth-shan. Some of these Cisjordan Valley sites were large, and, despite the silence of the Bible, must have been well known in their day. Others, of course, the Bible could not be expected to mention even vaguely, because they had ceased to exist several thousand years before its first pages were written.

Pass along the length of the west side of the Jordan and take notice of the large tells, which jut above the level of the landscape, many of them clearly visible from the eastern side. There is the massive Tell edh-Dhiabeh, looming over a widened section of the *Zor*, situated several hundred yards west of Jisr Sheikh Hussein, and anciently controlling both the way across the river and the pass leading to the Plain of Esdraelon. It is paralleled on the eastern side of the Jordan by a site almost equally large, called Tell Sheikh Mohammed, oc-

179

cupied especially in the eighteenth to seventeenth centuries B.C. A strong spring gives rise to a flowing stream, which irrigates the fields in front of Tell edh-Dhiabeh. Behind it to the west is a series of low ridges rising to the level of the Valley proper. The flattish top of the mound presents an extraordinary sight. Its surface is pock-marked with a maze of shallow pits, as though it had been invaded by an army of moles digging for cover and throwing up behind them all manner of objects. Around each pit we found a mass of fragments of brilliantly painted band-slip ware (Fig. 82). Many pieces were so large that even a tyro could visualize the complete pottery vessel to which they belonged. Large ledge-handles and fine pieces of pattern-burnished juglets were strewn about among numerous other sherds. The pottery picture was as clear as could be, representing a very distinctive period of settlement in Early Bronze I a, dating to the last quarter of the fourth millennium B.C. The pottery of Tell edh-Dhiabeh is not alone in its kind either in the Jordan Valley or elsewhere.

This pottery was characteristic of a widespread civilization which flowered for a few brief centuries. Finally some disaster overcame it, making desolate mounds of its inhabited hills, many of them never again to be settled. The ancient remains of Tell edh-Dhiabeh have been disturbed by *fellahin*, who stored their surplus grain in pits sunk into the dry earth on the top of the mound. They dug into a rich deposit of pottery, which had been left in the houses when they were destroyed in some terrible catastrophe. The pottery survived, because nothing short of crushing it into powder could make it unrecognizable, so enduring are well-baked wares.

A few hundred yards behind Tell edh-Dhiabeh, on a knoll to the west of it are pottery remains of a small Israelite settlement of the Early Iron Age. It had come into being some two thousand years after the Early Bronze Age site of Tell edh-Dhiabeh was destroyed. Beside it today has grown up the modern Jewish settlement of Maoz. The Israelite site has lost the name which distinguished it in Biblical times, and there are many others like it, deprived by time of their individual identities. There is, for instance, the small but strategically located Tell el-Mazar, which dominates the point where the widening Wadi el-Far'ah merges with the Jordan Valley. A perennial stream flows down this wadi, which in a small way parallels the larger river, Jabbok, on the opposite side of the Jordan. The sherds picked up on the slopes of Tell el-Mazar indicate that it was occupied in Israelite and pre-Israelite periods, as well as later, but there is no clue to its name in Biblical times. In the Jordan Valley, in the neighborhood of Beth-shan, there are numerous satellite towns, whose early identity likewise escapes us. It is possible, however, to fix the general periods of their occupation by the fragments of pottery found on them. North of Jericho, on the Wadi Auja et-Tahta and between the latter and Tell el-Mazar, are still other sites occupied in the Israelite period.

2

The anonymity which has cloaked almost all the ancient settlements on the west side of the Jordan, and whose importance, to our way of thinking, might well have warranted their being mentioned in the Bible, did not extend, fortunately, to its two outstanding cities. They were Beth-shan in the north, and Jericho in the south. These names have been preserved throughout the millenniums, down to our own day, when the Arabs still call them Beisan and er-Riha. Even the strong fortress of Hazor, which overlooked the west side of the Jordan River, south of Lake Huleh, and which was put to the sword and burnt by Joshua (Josh. 11:10, 11), could compare to neither of them.

The situation of Beth-shan was such that any settlement located there had to become the leading city of an important district. Several strong springs and the waters of the perennial Jalud irrigate a fertile soil into rich fecundity. The climate is subtropical. The outstanding mound, known today as Tell el-Husn, the "Fortress Hill," dominates the Jordan Valley at one of its widest and most fruitful parts (Fig. 83). It guards the Jordan end of the great highway which, following the length of the Plain of Esdraelon, connects the Mediterranean coast and the Nile valley with Mesopotamia. The counterpart of this

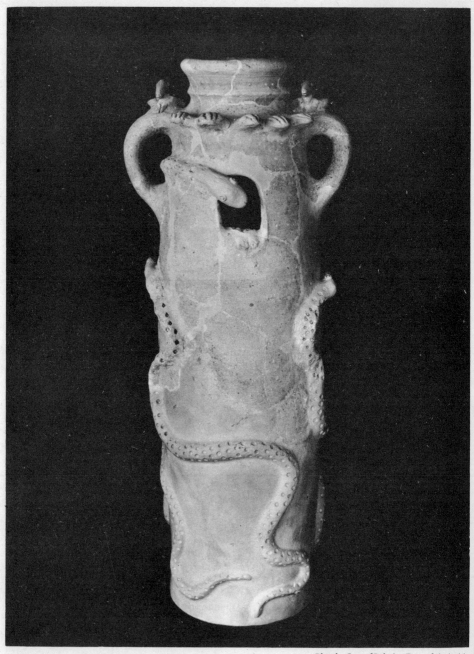

Photo by Govt. of Palestine, Dept. of Antiquities

FIG. 84. Twelfth century B.C. serpent jar from Beth-shan.

Fig. 85. Byzantine mosaic floor of Monastery of Lady Mary at Beth-shan: Scythopolis, showing months of November and December.

Fig. 86. Vintage scene on mosaic floor of 6th century A.D. Byzantine church at Beth-shan: Scythopolis.

FIG. 87. Pottery coffin of 12th century B.C. from
Beth-shan, made by Aegean mercenaries there.

Photo by Govt. of Palestine, Dept. of Antiquities

FIG. 88. Hieroglyphic inscription of Sethos I, from end of 14th century B.C., found at Beth-shan. It describes the nipping in the bud of a revolt in the Beth-shan area against Egyptian rule.

FIG. 89. Basalt statue of Ramesses III, of 12th century B.C.,
found at Beth-shan.

great fortress near the western end of the highway was the stronghold of Megiddo, later known as Armageddon and now called Tell
el-Mutesellim.

It is like turning the pages of a thoroughly documented and fas-
cinatingly interesting book of history to follow the course of the excavations which were conducted at Tell el-Husn. Beneath more
modern accumulations were found the ruins of the period of the
Crusades, during which the town was so thoroughly destroyed that
thereafter it never regained its former prosperity. The present Arab
village of Beisan, a short distance from the tell, is a poor successor to
the proud cities which preceded it, superimposed upon each other on
the original hill site. Beneath the Crusaders' masonry lay the fallen
fort, mosque, and dwellings of the Arabs, who completed their conquest of the entire land in A.D. 640, a few years after the death of
Mohammed in A.D. 632. The never forgotten ancient name of Beth-
shan then replaced the comparatively new name of Scythopolis, by
which it had been known to the Greeks and Romans. That name may
perhaps hark back to the seventh century B.C., when the warlike
Scythians of Indo-European origin, originally at home on the plains
of southern Russia, swept southward as far as the boundaries of
Egypt. It has been suggested that the name "Beth-shan" means the
"Temple of the Serpent-god." Be that as it may, among the most
interesting finds there were numerous representations of serpents,
one with human breasts and a milk bowl placed beneath them (Fig.
84). Beth-shan may have been a center of the serpent cult, which was
widespread in ancient Palestine. One recalls the serpent stele found
by Albright at Tell Beit Mirsim (Kiriath-sefer or Debir) in south-
western Palestine, and the presence of the Nehushtan, the copper
serpent, in Solomon's Temple in Jerusalem.

The Arabic buildings were found to have been built over the
curved walls and mosaic floors of a magnificent circular cathedral.
Underneath it were the remains of a rectangular basilica of early
Christian times. Across the valley, north of the tell, was a Byzantine
monastery with elaborate mosaic floors, featuring many kinds of
birds and a complex representation of the zodiac (Fig. 85). The

Christian buildings (Fig. 86) had replaced pagan temples of the Roman and still earlier Hellenistic periods. Among the ruins of these temples were the remains of one dating to the second–third centuries B.C., which was probably dedicated to the god Dionysus. Indeed, the town was sometimes named Nysa after his birthplace. In the year 107 B.C., the Jewish high priest John Hyrcanus gained control of Scythopolis. It remained under Maccabaean rule until 64 B.C., when Palestine became a Roman province. Under the Romans the city flourished mightily. It soon became the chief city of the Decapolis, that league of ten cities with Greco-Roman culture, among which we have already mentioned Gadara, Pella, Gerasa, and Philadelphia. The existing ruins of Gerasa (Jerash) help us to visualize what Hellenistic-Roman Scythopolis, Gadara, Jericho, Caesarea Philippi, and other contemporary cities looked like.

In earlier centuries the Philistines and Israelites had fought bitterly for possession of the vitally strategic point of Beth-shan, as it was then known. For a while, toward the end of the eleventh century B.C., the Philistines won out. It was then that "they put his [Saul's] armor in the temple of Ashtaroth and fastened his body to the wall of Beth-shan" (I Sam. 31:10). Subsequently, however, the Israelites seized the site and held it for several centuries.

The deepest imprint upon Beth-shan was left there by the Egyptians, who controlled Palestine during the second half of the second millennium B.C. Anthropoid sarcophagi (Fig. 87), made in imitation of Egyptian originals, have been found there. A whole series of Egyptian temples, inscriptions (Fig. 88), and statues (Fig. 89) has been found at Beth-shan in levels belonging to the period of Egyptian occupation, demonstrating how strong an interest the Egyptians had in the city. But Beth-shan was a cosmopolitan center, and other cultural influences were at play there, even during the time when Egyptian influence was predominant. Northern Syrian or northern Mesopotamian influence is represented by the lion relief from the Mekal temple belonging to about the fourteenth century B.C. (Fig. 90). An ax (Fig. 91) and dagger of Hittite design, Syro-Hittite cylinder seals, and a small bronze figure that seems to represent Teshub,

the Hittite storm-god, suggest Hittite influence during the period of
Ramesses II, in the thirteenth century B.C.

The excavations have shown that the site was already settled in the
late Chalcolithic period, at approximately 3500 B.C. (Fig. 92), that is,
more than five thousand years ago, and was continuously inhabited
after that. Flip the pages and get a moving-picture impression of the
actors crossing the stage of history at Beth-shan (Figs. 93, 94).
Among them were Canaanites, Egyptians (Fig. 95), Hittites, Babylonians, Philistines, Israelites, Scythians, Persians, Greeks, Romans,
Byzantines, Arabs, and Crusaders. And remember, the play has just
begun!

3

Of the two cities Beth-shan and Jericho, the latter has become the
more famous. History was at home there. The story of civilization
might well start with the words: "And in the beginning there was
Jericho." It stood at the edge of the hills (Fig. 96), in the midst of
fragrant gardens and verdant fields, irrigated into glowing greenness
by the unfailing waters of the Wadi Qelt. Immediately below the rise
on which it stood was the very strong spring, now known as 'Ain es-
Sultan and also as Elisha's fountain. Lordly palms afforded abundant
shade and succulent fruit in season. Groves of fat fig trees flourished,
and a heady wine was made of grapes ripening early in the subtropical heat. I have on a December day sat and soaked up the sun-
shine in Jericho, and then driven to Jerusalem an hour later to shiver
in the wintry blasts at large there. Nothing has ever grown in the
weird crisscross of chalky *qattarah* hills, which form a cruel belt of
no man's land between the carefully planted acres of the Plain of
Jericho and the wild Jungle of the Jordan below it.

Jericho drew men to it like a magnet. The goddess of the moon, to
whom it was early dedicated, blessed it with unrestrained bounty. Its
citizens grew rich and rotund. Its women flowered fast and married
young. It is true that they withered early, like tender grass under the
glare of a burning sun, but while their youth and strength lasted they
spent them prodigally. Their main pride lay in the sons they moth-

ered. Of daughters there was always a sufficiency for all purposes, for wives and fieldworkers, for concubines and courtesans. The trade of the latter was less sicklied over with sanctity than that of their sisters who functioned as sacred prostitutes in the shrines of Astarte. To the unhallowed guild of women for hire belonged Rahab. She plied her trade in her house on top of the great mud-brick wall which engirded the fullness of the rich Canaanite city of Jericho. How were the ponderous elders to know that in her frail hands would someday lie its destiny?

A crisis familiar to its past history once again confronted Jericho. Its pattern was known even to the children there. Had they not from infancy onward been frightened by tales of the wild men from the east who rode out of the desert like a fiery wind to ravage and plunder, to destroy and to burn? Always behind the opulence of Jericho lurked the fear of the raiders from Arabia, attracted to its riches like flies to honey. Their lean hunger could never be fattened, and their appetite seemed to grow with feeding. The chronicles of Jericho were replete with accounts of beating them back, buying them off, or being overwhelmed by them. More often than one cared to recall, they had come with careful calculation just at harvesttime and had besieged the city until they had filled their bellies with the grain they had neither sown nor reaped, eaten the fruit of trees they had not tended, and carried off what they could not consume. They would then retreat into the desert fastnesses where they could not be followed, leaving behind them the taunting assurance that they would return again in yet another year.

The danger that threatened Jericho this time was the most serious within the memory of any of its inhabitants. This was not the usual enemy that launched a sudden attack and then beat as sudden a retreat. This was an inundating flood. Would the walls of Jericho be sufficiently strong to stem it? Counsel was taken. Increased stores of food were stocked. All available fighting men were gathered together. The defenses of the great mud-brick wall were examined, and, where necessary, repaired and strengthened. Thousands of bricks were required for the purpose (Fig. 97). There was a flurry of activity

Fig. 90. Lion-dog panel, dating to 14th century B.C., from Beth-shan.

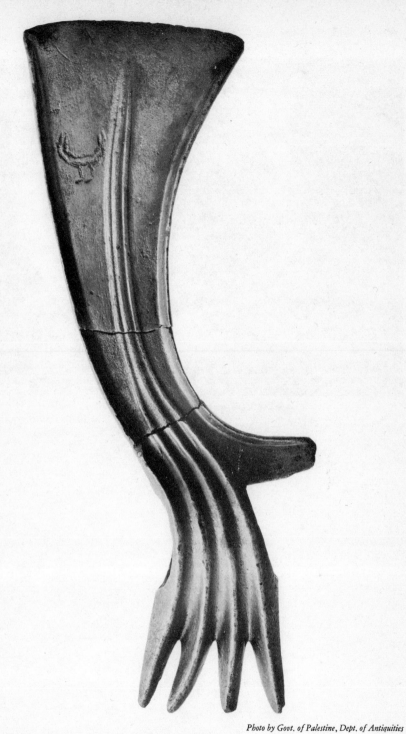

Photo by Govt. of Palestine, Dept. of Antiquities

FIG. 91. A 14th century B.C. Hittite battle-ax from Beth-shan. It is in the form of a stylized hand, with ornamental fingers continuing in raised lines almost to the bit. The knuckles enfold the handle's socket pierced through the breadth of the hand.

Photo by Govt. of Palestine, Dept. of Antiquities, and E. L. Sukenik, Museum of Jewish Antiquities, Jerusalem

FIG. 92. A highly polished, gray burnished pot from Beth-shan, dating about 2500 B.C.

FIG. 93. Face of old man modeled on neck of
13th century B.C. jar from Beth-shan.

Photo by Govt. of Palestine, Dept. of Antiquities

FIG. 94. Profiles painted on pottery from 14th century B.C. Beth-shan. The one on the left is a female; the one on the right, a male. The heads are filled in with red, while the outlines and details are in black.

FIG. 95. Head of pottery figurine of an Egyptian king, from Beth-shan, dating to about the 12th century B.C.

as mud was mixed with straw and pressed into rectangular wooden forms, and as the completed bricks were set out, row upon row, to dry in the sun (Fig. 98). But it was all in vain. The city was doomed, by treachery from within, by strategy and strength from without. There was to be no withstanding of the Bene-Israel, waiting on the other side of the Jordan for the signal to advance.

Their commander, Joshua ben-Nun, encamped at (Abel) Shittim in the Plains of Moab, at the northeast end of the Dead Sea, which could be seen across the river from Jericho, had sent out two men to look over the land and reconnoiter Jericho itself. They had found their way to the house of the harlot Rahab. Theirs was a dangerous mission, and what better hide-out in the town itself, and where better could they make inquiries about it, than in her home? Rahab yielded her favors for reward, and grabbed her gain where she could find it. She bore no love in her heart for her townsmen, who used her in private and avoided her in public. And would she ever forget the whispers of their wives and children, which often reached her ears as she passed them: "There goes Rahab the harlot"! She hated them all. The time had come when she could both have her revenge and save her skin. The two spies were speedily traced to her house. She hid them under the flax spread out to dry on its flat roof, while she sent their pursuers on a wild-goose chase after them to the fords of the Jordan. "Yes, the men came unto me, but I knew not whence they were: and it came to pass about the time of the shutting of the gate, when it was dark, that the men went out; whither the men went I know not: pursue after them quickly; for ye will overtake them. . . . And the men pursued after them the way to the Jordan unto the fords" (Josh. 2:4–7).

Earthy woman of the world that she was, Rahab was well-informed of the progress of the Bene-Israel through Transjordan, and she was convinced that nothing could stay their advance and that Jericho must fall before them, as all the other cities which lay in their path. Back she sped to the roof, to make her terms with the two strangers, whose lives were now in bond to her. She would help them to escape, if they would guarantee to save her life and the lives of her family when Jericho fell to the Israelite army. "I know," the Biblical account reports her as saying, "that the Lord hath given you the land, and that the fear of you is fallen upon us, and that all the inhabitants of the land melt away before you. We have heard how the Lord dried up the water of the Red Sea before you, . . . and what ye did to the two kings of the Amorites, that were beyond the Jordan, unto Sihon and Og, whom ye utterly destroyed. . . . For the Lord your God, he is God in heaven above, and on earth beneath" (vs. 9–11). The men agreed. "Our life for yours," they said, "if ye utter not this our business" (v. 14), and they gave her a scarlet cord to put in her window as token of security for her household, when the attack came. "Then she let them down by a rope through the window: for her house was upon the wall, and she dwelt upon the wall" (v. 15).

Excitement ran high in the camp of the Bene-Israel on the east side of the Jordan. With considerable anxiety, Joshua awaited the return of his two scouts. His people were ready to march. It would not do to delay the attack much longer. Death and hunger and weariness had long been their familiar companions. That was now all behind them. The struggle to reach the Jordan was still a subject for campfire re-telling, but no more than that. Finally Joshua received the intelligence report about Jericho for which he had sent his scouts. It was favorable to his plans. The inhabitants were frightened and dispirited. There were friends within the city itself. So forward, warriors of Israel! The tents were struck. The whole camp moved. The host reached the Jordan, the priests with the Ark in advance. And then the wonder occurred. The river became dammed up, ceasing to flow from Adamah southward. The people of Israel passed over on dry land. Taking twelve stones out of its bed, they set them up in Gilgal, on the west side of the Jordan facing Jericho, as a memorial of this divinely blessed adventure.

The news of the crossing of the Jordan had filled the inhabitants of Jericho with terror. "Now Jericho was straitly shut up because of the Bene-Israel: none went out, and none came in" (ch. 6:1). The strategy of the defenders was to sit tight and trust to the massive defenses of their great city wall. Should the enemy approach too closely, he would be showered with arrows and darts, and burned with boiling oil in case he ventured still nearer. But the tactics of the invaders were of a different order. For six days they encircled the city, while the weakhearted there grew faint with fear and internal dissension mounted apace. Clamorous grew the cries for submission while there was yet time, for coming to terms with the Israelites who were crowned with the halo of invincibility, and whose march westward had been marked by one miracle after another.

Meanwhile Rahab sat secure in her house. One by one she had gathered her family to her perch, whispering to each: "There is no hope for you save in my care. There is no hope." And soon the whisper was echoed in every house and had penetrated the fastness of every heart: "There is no hope. There is no hope." The battle was really over before it had begun. The Bene-Israel had but to batter at the gates and the great bastion would fall like an overripe fig. Indeed, this was the order of the battle for the seventh day. The priests were to blow the trumpets, and the people to shout great shouts, and, under the intoxication of the tumult, to attack. The conclusion was a foregone one. Jericho was bound to fall. The stars were set in their courses against her. The very earth was disturbed to its depths. It trembled, and the firm wall of Jericho fell flat. Its bricks had been too beautifully bonded together to allow any leeway for waves of motion released by tremors not uncommon in that region. The city was suddenly bared even of all semblance of defense.

"And it came to pass, when the people heard the sound of the trumpet, that the people shouted with a great shout, and the wall fell down flat, so that the people went up into the city, every man straight before him, and they took the city" (v. 20). Mindful of the promise to Rahab, they brought her and her family to safety outside of the camp of Israel, whereupon "they burnt the city with fire" (v. 24). "And Joshua charged them with an oath at that time, saying, Cursed be the man before the Lord, that riseth up and buildeth this city of Jericho: with the loss of his first-born shall he lay its foundations, and with the loss of his youngest son shall he set up its gates" (v. 26).

So once again Jericho was destroyed, as it had been so often in its long history. A veritable Babel's tower of towns had sprung up over the original knoll by the time of the last Canaanite city, which the treacherous Rahab betrayed. The most recent ruins were soon mercifully buried under a thin cover of dirt brought by the winds. For several centuries no new town was built on top of the tell, until finally, in the ninth century B.C., Hiel of Beth-el braved Joshua's ban and suffered the consequences of his curse. "In his [Ahab's] days did Hiel the Beth-elite rebuild Jericho. He laid its foundations with the loss of Abiram his first-born, and set up its gates with the loss of his youngest son Segub, according to the word of the Lord, which he spake by Joshua ben-Nun" (I Kings 16:34).

Delving deeply into the mound of ancient Jericho, known today as Tell es-Sultan, archaeologists have found remains reaching back for many millenniums. In one sector, at the northeast corner, they dug through eighty feet of the debris of seventeen settlements before sterile soil was reached. Starting at the top and going downward in space and backward in time, the strata of these settlements have been numbered from I to XVII. They carry the history of man at Jericho from the thirteenth century B.C. almost as far back as the Natufian period of the Mount Carmel caves. Combining the evidence of the two places, one can sketch an outline of man's activities in Palestine for a period of over one hundred thousand years.

The first settlers at Jericho left behind them very delicate, tiny flints, which are called microliths. These minute blades and other tools required the most careful craftsmanship, and could not possibly have withstood hard usage. Just exactly how they were employed—whether they were inserted in wooden grooves to form sawlike blades or were otherwise used—remains a mystery. The stages of expanding civilization were now to succeed each other rapidly. It was not long before those who followed the microlith makers learned to build permanent houses of considerable excellence. Seven successive floors, composed of clay and lime, pounded firm, and painted and polished dull red, are all that remain from the structures of these houses. Each house in turn, after its destruction,

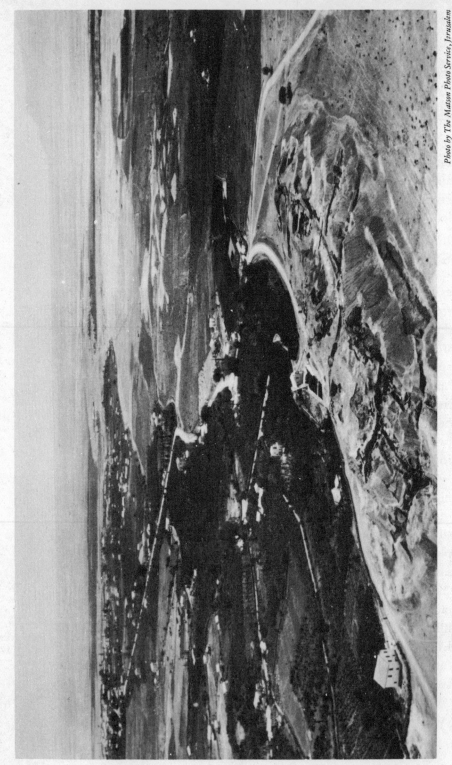

Photo by The Matson Photo Service, Jerusalem

FIG. 96. The excavated mound of Tell es-Sultan, ancient Jericho, in the foreground. Beyond it, the gardens and Plain of Jericho, with a view toward the Dead Sea.

Photo by American Schools of Oriental Research

FIG. 97. Unused bricks from brickyard at ancient Ezion-geber, Solomon's seaport on the eastern arm of the Red Sea. Hidden under debris, these sun-dried mud bricks remained intact after an interval of almost 3,000 years.

Photo by American Schools of Oriental Research

Fig. 98. Present-day manufacture of sun-dried mud bricks at Aqabah, Transjordan.

Photos by Govt. of Palestine, Dept. of Antiquities

FIG. 99. (*a*) Shell-eyed head of neolithic cult-statue from Jericho, modeled in clay about 7,000 years ago.

(*b*) Profile of shell-eyed head of neolithic cult statue from Jericho.

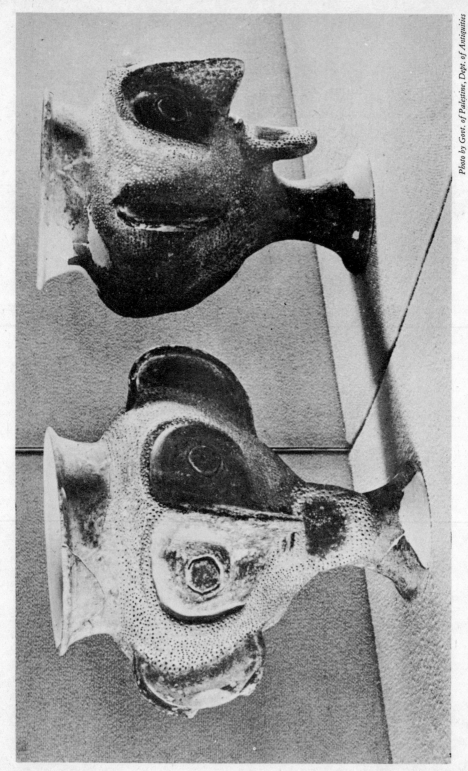

FIG. 100. "Jericho John" and his mirrored profile. An anthropomorphic vase from 17th century B.C. Jericho.

FIG. 101. Zeus-Hadad, from Nabataean temple
of Khirbet Tannur, Transjordan.

served as a foundation for the one subsequently built upon it. By the time the walls of the topmost one collapsed, there had been added to the original height of the mound some 20 feet of debris, consisting of strata XVII–IX.

In stratum XI there were some small clay figurines of goats and sheep and other domesticated animals. Were they toys, or were they symbols of some early fertility cult? In stratum IX, which may be attributed to about 5000 B.C., and extending down into X, was found an instructive clay model of a house. It looked like a beehive, with a rounded conical roof of the type that can be seen today in some parts of Syria and Mesopotamia. With a floor of stone slabs over a thick base, it was 40 inches high and 30 inches wide. A doorway was meant to be closed by rolling a round, flat stone into place. There was a second story occupying the upper third of the building, supported by a central pillar, with another pillar supporting the domed roof.

These houses were a far cry from the cave dwellings of the Paleolithic period, but an even farther cry was the sculptor's atelier in stratum X, in which some amazing works of art remained. It is true that the medium was clay, that the technique was crude, that the product was primitive, but the sculptor fashioned his figures with artistic imagination and power. They were built up on a framework of reeds. One head in particular has been preserved almost intact. It was formed to show the full face. One forgets, when looking at it, that the head is actually flat, having little more depth than necessary to mold the face. The sightless stillness of the deeply impressed shell eyes, the ridged eyebrows, aquiline nose, prominent cheeks, lines of paint representing tattooing or hair, or both, and the thin line of mouth above a somewhat protruding lower lip, combine to lend a quality of impersonal, but strong reality to this primitive sculpture. It is like a death mask of someone who had been vibrantly alive (Figs. 99a, b). Remains of a pair of legs, one of them bent gracefully at the knee, were also recovered. It is not impossible, although it seems unlikely, that the flat, shell-eyed head was part of the same feminine (?) figure, to which these legs, modeled in the round, belonged. Two groups of sculptures were found, representing apparently an early triad of god and goddess and offspring. It must be remembered that these figures were fashioned about 5000 B.C.! Civilization was developing by leaps and bounds in the Jordan Valley. Not long thereafter, highly complex and brilliantly ornate frescoes with religious themes were painted at the near-by Chalcolithic settlement of Teleilat Ghassul.

The artist who created the shell-eyed figures in Jericho was kin to the craftsman who made sun-dried pottery there, mixed with straw as a binder. Bricks too were formed in this fashion. In a much later age, Israelite slaves in Egypt were to find their burden completely unbearable when Pharaoh refused to give them straw for the bricks they were forced to provide for his building projects. Already in stratum IX attempts were made to bake pottery in kilns. From then on it rapidly improved, changing sufficiently as each age passed by to enable it to become an index of history. By the Middle Bronze Age, which covers the first half of the second millennium B.C., it achieved an excellence which was never to be surpassed in later Palestine.

There is a remarkable vase from Jericho belonging to the seventeenth century B.C. The potter turned on his wheel a graceful carinated, trumpet-foot vase, typical of the period, and then fashioned it by hand into the likeness of one of his contemporaries, and baked it into a monument to his memory, which has endured now for thousands of years. The representation is highly stylized, but the exaggerated eyebrows, large round eyes incised after baking, nose protruding like a wedge-shaped blade from the forehead, full lips, spade beard, ears extended to form handles, hair on face and of beard indicated by pinholes, unmistakably portray a sharply intelligent, quizzically energetic Semite (Fig. 100). The vase has been nicknamed "Jericho John" by irreverent archaeologists, because of the supposed likeness to Professor John Garstang, the excavator of Jericho.

A glowing description of the fruitful oasis of Jericho is given by Josephus (*The Jewish War*, IV:viii.3). "There is a fountain by Jericho, that runs plentifully. . . . The report is, that this fountain, at the beginning, caused not only the blasting of the earth and the trees, but of the children born of women, . . . but that it was made gentle, and very wholesome and fruitful, by the prophet Elisha. . . . It . . . passes along a plain . . . wherein it affords nourishment to those most excellent gardens that are thick set with trees. There are in it many sorts of palm trees that are watered by it, different from each other in taste and name. . . . This country withal produces honey from bees; it also bears that balsam which is the most precious of all the fruits in that place, cypress trees also. . . . He who should pronounce this place to be divine would not be mistaken. . . . It will not be easy to light on any climate in the habitable earth that can well be compared to it." The fertility of the plains of Jericho and Beth-shan has continued undiminished. At the time of the Crusades, there were sugar-cane plantations at both places.

No wonder Joshua's troops and their families looked with eager eyes on this earthly paradise. They coveted it and conquered it. And then the years were to run away, like sand pouring out of an hour-glass. In time Saul became king of Israel, only to fall in battle before the Philistines and have his body impaled on the wall of Beth-shan. David hung up his lyre, seized the scepter of kingship and ruled firmly with cunning and sometimes cold-blooded hand, though often racked with fierce passions and fiercer griefs. Solomon succeeded him, and raised Israel by his genius to a position of power and importance without parallel in its earlier or later history. Israel shone in Solomon's glory, at the expense of having foisted upon it a despotic Oriental monarchy. The evil that Solomon did lived after him. Much of the good perished with his passing. His painfully built-up kingdom was split lastingly asunder after his death. Israel and Judah parted company, to succumb separately to foreign forces. Having wasted much of their strength in mutual enmity, they were easily overrun, Israel by Assyria at the end of the eighth century B.C., and Judah by Babylonia near the beginning of the sixth century B.C.

4

Look at the mob fleeing in wild disorder along the road from Jerusalem to Jericho. It consists of the army, or rather the remnants of the army, of the king of Judah, which had been worsted in battle

against the Babylonians. Zedekiah had raised his hand in reckless rebellion against Babylon, and now he was a fugitive from Jerusalem.
He had ruled there merely by sufferance because Babylon had already established its power over Palestine. He had sought now to
rule in freedom and by right, as others had before him. He had
gambled and lost. Now to escape, if possible, to the hills on the
other side of the Jordan, or farther even into the reaches of the desert,
whence the Bene-Israel had once emerged. But it was not to be! The
Judeans had almost reached the green gardens of Jericho, where they
had hoped to find at least a brief respite, when the pursuing Babylonian troops overtook them. Among the prisoners were the king
and the young princes, who were carried to the camp of Nebuchadnezzar. Cruel vengeance was to be exacted. The Chaldean monarch
would now make it absolutely clear that he indeed was the master of
Palestine and was not to be trifled with. He would have his pleasure
of these captives. Executioners unsheathed their swords. A fire was
kindled, and iron rods were placed in it. A nod, and the stupefied
children were slain in front of their father. The light went out of his
face. What mattered it now that he was grasped tightly, while the
glowing metal was pressed first against one eyeball and then against
the other, scarring them sightless!

"Zedekiah rebelled against the king of Babylon. . . . Thereupon,
Nebuchadnezzar king of Babylon came, he and his army, against
Jerusalem, encamped against it, and built a siege wall around it. . . .
The city wall was breached, and the king fled. . . . But the army of
the Chaldeans pursued after the king, and overtook him in the plains
of Jericho. . . . They slew the sons of Zedekiah before his eyes,
blinded him, bound him in chains, and brought him to Babylon"
(II Kings 24:20 to 25:1–7).

Thus ended the history of the first kingdom of Judah. The wheel
had turned a full revolution. The path from Jericho to Jerusalem and
back again had proved to be a short one. Joshua's people were again
crossing the Jordan, but this time eastward into exile, to sing songs
of loneliness by the rivers of Babylon. However, the soil of Palestine
had entered into their souls, and they were never again able to sever

FIG. 102. Zeus (?) head from Khirbet Tannur.

Fig. 103. Atargatis, as grain goddess, from Khirbet Tannur.

FIG. 104. Western (Wailing) Wall of the Temple built in Jerusalem by Herod the Great.

Photo by Govt. of Palestine, Dept. of Antiquities

Photo by Govt. of Palestine, Dept. of Antiquities

Fig. 105. Herodium. Ruins of the fortress, built by Herod the Great, guarding the road to the Dead Sea.

Fig. 106. Looking down at craterlike, artificial top of Herodium (Frank Mountain), built by Herod the Great.

themselves from it. "We sat by the waters of Babylon, and wept when we thought of Zion. . . . If I forget thee, O Jerusalem, may my right hand fail me. May my tongue cleave to the roof of my mouth, if I do not hold thee in remembrance, if I set not Jerusalem above my highest joy" (Ps. 137:1–6). God had walked abroad in the Promised Land and had made his voice heard. Prophets and priests and the lowliest shepherds had listened, and the message has remained imprinted in the hearts of commoners and kings. The waters of the Jordan thenceforth laved a land, from which the Torah, the Teaching of the Lord, was continuously to go forth. Palestine became spiritually what the facts of geography had made it physically, the focal point of the world, with Jerusalem its central city and the Jordan the world's central stream.

5

Palestine's blessing and curse lie in its geographical position, which makes it a bridge between the nations. It is a crossroads on the deathless trade routes between East and West. Its strategic importance in more recent times has been recognized and fought over by Richard the Lionhearted and Saladin, by Napoleon and Nelson, by Allenby and Liman von Sanders, by Wavell and Rommel. It stands today between England and India, between America and Arabia, whose desert sands cover an ocean of oil. Britain is at present in control, but others are reaching out for empire.

With regard to Palestine, the great geopolitical pathfinder, Halford J. Mackinder, writes as follows: "In a monkish map, contemporary with the Crusades, which still hangs in Hereford Cathedral, Jerusalem is marked as the geometrical center of the world, and on the floor of the Church of the Holy Sepulchre in Jerusalem, they will show you till this day the precise spot which is the center. If our study of the geographical realities, as we now know them in completeness, is leading us to right conclusions, the medieval ecclesiastics were not far wrong. If the World-Island be inevitably the principal seat of humanity on this globe, and if Arabia, as the passage land from Europe to the Indies and from the Northern to the

Southern Heartland, be central in the World-Island, then the hill-citadel of Jerusalem has a strategical position with regard to world realities not differing essentially from its ideal position in the perspective of the Middle Ages, or its strategical position between ancient Babylon and Egypt. As the war has shown, the Suez Canal carries the rich traffic between the Indies and Europe to within striking distance of an army based on Palestine, and already the trunk railway is being built [has been built] through the coastal plain by Jaffa, which will connect [connects] the Southern with the Northern Heartland."[1] To this one might add: He who holds Jerusalem and the Jordan in his heart holds the world in his hands. "Who shall ascend the hill of the Lord? and who shall stand in his holy place? He that hath clean hands, and a pure heart; who hath not lifted up his soul to falsehood, nor sworn deceitfully. He shall receive a blessing from the Lord, and righteousness from the God of salvation. This is the generation of them that seek thee, that seek thy face, O God of Jacob" (Ps. 24: 3–6).

6

Before being banished in large numbers to Babylonia, the Judeans had been rooted in Palestine for seven centuries. Many of those who had been torn from what had for so long been their ancestral home seized the very first opportunity to return. When their conquerors succumbed to the power of Persia, its kings gave these early Zionists permission to go up again to the Promised Land. With the active assistance of Cyrus and Darius in the latter part of the sixth century B.C., and of Artaxerxes I about the middle of the fifth, they made increasingly successful efforts to resettle in Judah, rebuild the walls of Jerusalem, restore the Temple, and re-establish the community according to the theocratic concepts they had mulled over while away. Among "the citizens whom Nebuchadnezzar, king of Babylon, had carried away to Babylon, and [who] returned to Jerusalem and Judah, each to his city," are listed 345 inhabitants of Jericho (Ezra 2:1, 34). How glad they must have been to see their city of palms again, how

[1] *Democratic Ideals and Reality*, p. 89.

delighted their children born abroad must have been with it! There were changes, to be sure. Among the chief of them was the fact, to which they themselves were to contribute, that vernacular Hebrew was giving way to Aramaic. The Book of Ezra, which recorded their history, was composed partly in that dialect.

7

Change followed change in Palestine and Transjordan, and naturally also in the Jordan Valley. After the Persians came the Greeks. And Greek influence was in many ways the most important and fateful that had ever spread across the land. With method and persistence Alexander the Great (333–323 B.C.) and the generals who succeeded him carried out the Hellenization of most of the Near East. Greek influence spread as far south as Arabia and as far east as India. I have excavated black glazed Greek sherds of the fourth century B.C. at Ezion-geber (Elath) on the north shore of the east arm of the Red Sea. I have found at Khirbet Tannur in southern Transjordan a Nabataean altar bearing in Greek characters the composite Greco-Semitic name of its donor, Alexandros Amrou. There too I have dug up Nabataean gods whose images were hardly distinguishable from figures of Zeus (Figs. 101, 102), Atargatis (Fig. 103), Helios, and Tyche elsewhere in the Hellenistic world. These were the gods worshiped also in the Hellenistic-Roman temples in such places as Caesarea Philippi, Beth-shan, Gadara, and Pella. They were thus also well known throughout the Jordan Valley. Jews like Hillel preached the love of God in a world where the gods of love and fertility were commonly familiar.

I have picked up a Rhodian jar handle on an ancient site in the Jordan Valley. It could be dated by the name of a Greek eponym impressed on it in the first part of the second century B.C. At that time the Greek garrisons and settlements scattered through Palestine and Transjordan preferred the resinated wine imported from the island of Rhodes to the local products. From the great Greek metropolis of Alexandria, which for a long period was to be the greatest city in the world, and from the capital established by Seleucus at Antioch on the

Orontes, after the death of Alexander, powerful streams of Greek cultural influence converged upon Palestine.

If Greeks came to Palestine, Jews returned the compliment and went abroad in great numbers, of their own free will. The Jewish community in Alexandria, living under the Ptolemaic dynasty, which controlled Palestine from 301 to 198 B.C., became so large, and so well assimilated to its Greek environment, that its members could no longer read the Bible in the original Hebrew. A Greek translation, the Septuagint, came into being, parts of it being completed by the middle of the third century B.C. Greek philosophy influenced some Jewish writings. The Jewish poet Philo wrote an epic poem on Jerusalem in Greek. Much of the literature of the New Testament was written in Greek. Other Jewish documents, written originally in Aramaic or Hebrew, have been preserved only in Greek translations. For three centuries before, and for centuries after the time of Christ, Greek influence predominated in greater Palestine, manifesting itself steadily during the Roman and Byzantine periods. Nevertheless, the country remained Hebraic at core, stubbornly proud of its prophetic and priestly traditions.

This became apparent when Antiochus IV, known also as Antiochus Epiphanes, ascended the Syrian throne and made a violent attempt forcibly to Hellenize all of Judea. He belonged to the Seleucid dynasty established in Syria, which in 198 B.C. had replaced the Egyptian Ptolemies as the controlling power over Palestine. It became a fundamental part of his policy to turn the Jews away from the Lord, and to make them identify themselves completely with Greek culture in all its aspects. But he was to find the Jews a stiff-necked people, who persisted in worshiping in their own way, regardless of consequences. He forbade circumcision and the observance of the Sabbath under penalty of death. He made pagan sacrifices on the part of the Jews obligatory, and attempted to force them to eat swine's flesh. Not content with plundering the Temple of many of its finest treasures, he set up an altar dedicated to Olympian Zeus on the sacred altar of burnt offering in the Temple itself. This occurred in the year 168 B.C. and set off a rebellion that had long been smoldering. Led by the Maccabees, a fitful freedom was achieved under the Hasmonaean dynasty, whose uneasy rule endured for little over a century. Then the government fell into the ruthlessly capable hands of Herod the Great. This occurred shortly after the death of his father, Antipater, who had been the real power behind the throne of the last Maccabean king, Hyrcanus II.

8

Throughout his long reign, from 37 to 4 B.C., Herod the Great proved to be a champion of the Jews, a friend of the Romans, and an admirer of the Greeks. In actual practice he was a dangerous despot who feared for his position, and bore down with murderous hand upon every possible source of uprising. He even had three of his own sons executed. No wonder Augustus was to say of him that it was better to be Herod's pig than his son. However, he maintained peace in Palestine, and that was what his Roman masters, to whom it had become subject, demanded above all from the governors of their provinces. Of all his domain he loved best the valley of the Jordan.

Herod was no uncouth provincial, but a well-traveled and highly cultured man who lived in a predominantly Greek part of the world under Roman dominion. He was a polished diplomat, who knew to a nicety how to gain the respect and friendship of a succession of Roman rulers, from Caesar through Mark Antony, Augustus, and Marcus Agrippa. Upon their favor depended his own weal and the welfare of his country and people. To each in turn Herod was wise enough to pay unwaveringly loyal fealty.

This cosmopolitan part Jew, whose mother was a Nabataean and whose father was of Idumaean extraction, was in effect one of the greatest ambassadors to the Gentiles that the Jews had ever had. During his reign, as a result of his wise statesmanship, no foreign armies pillaged Palestine. He was one of the few who resisted the lures of insatiable Cleopatra. She had already obtained parts of Arabia and the rich Jericho region as a gift from Mark Antony, who was as wax in her arms. Then she came to Jerusalem, scheming to trade her fleeting favors for the price of Herod's possessions. In him, however, she met her match. Indeed, Herod was minded to have her killed, as of advantage to Mark Antony and himself, but his council of friends dissuaded him. At least this is the story that Josephus would have us believe. So "he treated Cleopatra kindly, and made her presents, and conducted her on her way to Egypt," after having "farmed of her her parts of Arabia, and those revenues that came to her from the region about Jericho" (*The Jewish Antiquities*, XV:iv.2).

So far as his general education and outlook are concerned, Herod was more Greek than Jew. Like Solomon, whom he resembled in some respects, Herod had a passion for building. The peace he brought his country endowed it with a great prosperity and secured for himself great riches, with which he embarked on a vast public works program. He altered the very aspect of Jerusalem, making it an imposing Greco-Roman metropolis. His crowning achievement there was the construction of the third Temple (Fig. 104). It was, however, not completely finished till A.D. 63–64, many years after the death of Herod. Six years later the Romans destroyed it, after crushing the Jewish rebellion against them, and it was never again rebuilt. Herod's house of God was in form largely a Greek temple, a fact heightened by the golden eagle he had set up above its great gate. When a premature report of his death was broadcast, the eagle was pulled down, to the applause of the multitude. Josephus probably inferred correctly that the building of a resplendent Temple in Jerusalem by Herod stemmed less out of a sense of piety than from a desire to raise "an everlasting memorial" to himself (*The Jewish Antiquities*, XV:xi.1). Parts of the Herodian structure are still visible.

The magnificent edifices in Jerusalem represented, however, only a part of Herod's contribution to the architecture of Palestine. He built according to a master plan which made for the adornment, security, and general well-being of the country. In the Jordan Valley alone he built a string of fortresses and towns, stretching all the way from Jericho to Banias. "He also built a city . . . in the valley of Jericho, as you go from it northward, whereby he rendered the neighbouring country more fruitful by the cultivation its inhabitants introduced; and this also he called Phasaelus" (*The Jewish Antiquities*,

FIG. 107. Fortress of Masada, with remnants of Roman wall of circumvallation visible at the base of the hill.

Photo by S. J. Schweig, Jerusalem

FIG. 108. Base of hill of Masada, looking east across the Dead Sea, and showing ruins of Roman camp and wall of circumvallation.

XVI:v.2), in memory of his brother Phasaelus. To the north of it he rebuilt the towering Hasmonaean fortress of Alexandrium (Qarn Sartabeh), on top of a great hill which commands a view of much of the length of the Jordan Valley.

It was the city of Jericho, however, which received his special attention. He adorned it with a beautiful theater and a fine hippodrome. He also built a citadel there which he named Cyprus, in honor of his mother, and a tower, which he called Phasaelus after his brother. Herod loved his relatives when they were dead. The richness and warmth of the oasis of Jericho delighted Herod and soothed his nerves. Its remoteness from Jerusalem relieved his worries, for he was in constant fear, as every harsh dictator must be, for his personal safety. He spent his last days in Jericho, rotting away into a miserable death, like an overripe melon in the hot sun.

From Jerusalem it was but a few hours' chariot ride southeastward to the powerful fortress of Herodium (Fig. 105), which he had built anew and named after himself. It looks from the air like an extinct volcano (Fig. 106). Thence a direct track led down southeastward to the mighty, almost inaccessible bastion of Masada (Fig. 107), overlooking the Dead Sea (Fig. 108). He greatly strengthened this naturally strong fortress crag, making it practically impregnable. He also rebuilt the fortress of Machaerus, towering over the northeast side of the Dead Sea. From the Mediterranean to beyond the Jordan, Herod built a large number of powerful bastions. He sought thus to be secure from foreign enemies as well as from internal opposition and rebellion. He trusted neither Rome nor Jerusalem.

Herod was a child of his age. He did what the Caesars of Rome did. He lived up to, and in many respects surpassed, the standards by which they measured success. Had he been born in other times and under different conditions, he might well have eclipsed the emperors to whom he paid allegiance. As it is, Josephus quotes Augustus and Agrippa as saying, "The dominions of Herod were too little for the greatness of his soul; for that he deserved to have both all the kingdom of Syria, and that of Egypt also" (*The Jewish Antiquities*, XVI: v.1). His buildings, however, were soon shattered. His achievements hardly survived his death. For five thousand years before him men had been building palaces in places like Jericho, only to have their work dissolve like the evening dew in the morning sun. Heaps of rubble, piles of great blocks, fragments of tremendous walls, a few outstanding ruins, are all that remain, here and there in Palestine and Transjordan, of Herod's resplendent structures. As often as not, many of them are concealed under decrepit hovels and village dumps. But in their time his harbor works and fortresses, his hippodromes and temples, formed a crown of glory for Herod and for Palestine.

Listen to the flourish of trumpets, the roll of drums, the clash of cymbals, the clatter of a cavalcade. Run, citizens and slaves, patricians and shepherds, Jews and Greeks, run, to see the stirring spectacle! Marcus Agrippa, the emperor of Rome, has arrived! Yes, Marcus Agrippa himself! And with him, Herod, radiant, resplendent. Truly, these two do not make the appearance of master and servant, but of monarchs of equal rank—the imperious Agrippa and the dynamic Herod. Look, they are walking now, arm in arm, both smiling, and nodding graciously to the cheering throngs. Aye, clap hands, sound the joyous hallel, let song echo from wall to wall! Who can refrain from being swept away by the happy excitement, from forgetting his doubts about this pomp and pageantry in the cheer of the moment! "When Herod . . . understood that Marcus Agrippa had sailed again out of Italy into Asia, he made haste to him, and besought him to come . . . into his kingdom, and to partake of what he might justly expect from one that had been his guest, and was his friend. . . . Agrippa agreed, and came into Judea; whereupon Herod omitted nothing that might please him. . . . He . . . showed him . . . Sebaste and Cesarea . . . that port that he had built, and . . . the fortresses which he had erected at great expenses, Alexandrium, and Herodium, and Hyrcania. He also conducted him to the city Jerusalem, where all the people met him in their festival garments, and received him with acclamations" (*The Jewish Antiquities*, XVI:ii.1).

For days such as these, for the taste of this triumph, Herod had labored all his life. Who could fail to read Agrippa's countenance and see how amazed and pleased he was with Herod and his works, how appreciative of the peace which kept the channels of imperial trade open, how delighted he was with this cultured king of the Jews, who had brought Rome to Jerusalem. What Agrippa could not be expected to know and what Herod himself was hardly aware of, was the inner life of the people of the land. In the last analysis, the multitudes of simple, pious folk and the spiritual authorities they recognized were little touched by the majestic façades that Herod reared everywhere in the land. In spite of all the glitter of the Greek world about them, they adhered to the simple faith of their fathers.

9

There was, for instance, the gentle Jew, Rabbi Hillel, who lived in Jerusalem at the time of Herod. He was active from approximately 30 B.C. to A.D. 10, being the Nasi, prince of the Sanhedrin, and a recognized leader among his people. In him was incorporated, more than in any other man of his day, the spirit of the finest prophetic traditions. He was an exalted exponent of purest Judaism, which flowered unsullied in an environment where hedonistic Hellenism manifested itself so ostentatiously. Hillel was above all the great teacher, who preached and practiced the virtues of charity, humility, and real piety. He was a gigantic influence among his fellow Jews in his own generation, setting an inspired example for all men.

How well he knew the foibles of men, how insistently he urged that they be judged charitably! "Judge not thy neighbor until thou art in his place," he said (Aboth II:4). And a few years later another great Jew was to say: "Judge not, that ye be not judged. . . . And why beholdest thou the mote that is in thy brother's eye, but considerest not the beam that is in thine own eye?" (Matt. 7:1–3). When asked by a proselyte to teach him the Torah in the shortest possible form, Hillel replied: "What is unpleasant to thyself, that do not do to thy neighbor. This is the whole law, all else is but its exposition" (Shabbath 31a). Thus he evinced his intensely practical and deeply understanding way of explaining to the ordinary man the simple meaning of the Biblical injunction to love thy neighbor as thyself, which is contained in Lev. 19:18. And Jesus shortly thereafter was to say: "Whatsoever ye would that men should do unto you, even so do ye also unto them: for this is the law and the prophets" (Matt. 7:12). A rabbinical tradition relates that once when the sages were assembled at Jericho a heavenly voice was heard, saying: "Among those here present is one who would have deserved the Holy Spirit to rest upon him, if the age he lived in had been worthy of it. And all eyes turned toward Hillel" (Tosefta Sotah XIII:3).

10

In the same prophetic tradition Jesus continued to teach and interpret the Torah. Few in his generation were more familiar with its basic principles and enduring significance than this young Rabbi. He answered the lawyer's question as to how eternal life might be inherited by making him recall two Biblical passages, the one from Deut. 6:5, "Thou shalt love the Lord thy God with all thy heart, and with all thy soul, and with all thy might," and the other, "Thou shalt love . . . thy neighbor as thyself," which Hillel had quoted to the proselyte (Cf. Luke 10:25–27). With a parable, Jesus replied to the legalistic question as to the exact meaning of the word "neighbor" in this latter passage. A traveler on his way from Jerusalem to Jericho fell among thieves. A priest and a Levite passed him by, heedless of his hurt. Finally, a certain Samaritan succored him, and lodged him in a neighboring inn at his own expense (Fig. 109). The parable was ended. Was the point clear? "Which of these three," Jesus questioned his questioner, "proved neighbor unto him that fell among the robbers? And he [the lawyer] replied, He that showed mercy on him. Then Jesus said unto him, Go thou and do likewise" (Luke 10:36, 37).

How gay are the crowds that throng the roads leading southward through the Jordan Valley to Jericho! The people are happy. The land is green. Newborn lambs and goats skip and frolic. The planted fields, beribboned with irrigation streams, are bursting with fullness. Waves of color mark ripples of motion as heavy heads of grain bow before the press of the winds. Swallows and brilliantly hued bee eaters swoop about. Sweet smells fill the air. Lilting songs herald the coming

Fig. 109. The "Good Samaritan's Inn" beside the road, which runs through the Wilderness of Judah.

Photo by The Matson Photo Service, Jerusalem

FIG. 110. Mount of Temptation at Jericho, with the monastery below summit.

of the happy pilgrims. The time of Passover is almost at hand, and all who are able are hastening to Jerusalem, to break the unleavened wafer at festival supper there. Each community along the entire length of the Jordan Valley, and from beyond Jordan too, has contributed its quota of celebrants. They are making their joyful way to the mountain shrine of the city of peace, to give thank offerings for the first fruits of the season and for the freedom from bondage anciently obtained by their ancestors. A natural halting place was always at fabulous Jericho, the valley gateway to the hill fortress. Among the pilgrims is the Jew, Jesus, who is to become known as the Prince of Peace. His offering is to be a supreme one, the sacrifice of his life.

Rome ruled Palestine not only through its Pontius Pilates, but also through a small minority of royalist Jews. These fought among themselves for the fat crumbs of position and privilege that their masters threw them. Like their rulers, they resented and feared change, abhorred criticism and reproach. The like of these Romans and their puppets manifests itself in every generation and in every land. They had sneered at Amos in the high place at Beth-el. They had thrust Jeremiah into prison in Jerusalem and subjected him throughout his life to such indignities that he cursed the day he was born. Listen to the jackals howling for his life, when Jeremiah ventured to preach the word of God to his people. He said to them: "Thus saith the Lord: If ye will not hearken to me, to walk in my law, . . . I will make this house like Shiloh, and this city a curse to all the nations of the earth. . . . Then spake the priests and the [professional] prophets unto the princes, and to all the people, saying, This man is worthy of death" (Jer. 26:4–6, 11). And of Jesus, too, their like said later: "He is worthy of death" (Matt. 26:66). And so Jesus was crucified, as many other Jews who were accounted dangerous to the regime were crucified in his day.

From splendid Caesarea Philippi at the Banias source of the Jordan, Jesus journeyed to Capernaum by the Lake of Galilee, where he preached in the synagogue. Thence he went to Judah and beyond Jordan. Finally, he found his way back to the Jordan Valley, making halt, a few days before Passover, at Jericho. Herod the Great had transformed it into the likeness of a magnificent Roman city. And Jesus, perforce aware of the splendor of the palaces and the power of the princes in Jericho, must have reflected how pitiful and puny and transitory all this arrogant grandeur really was. He must already have entertained the thought to which, shortly afterward, he gave concrete expression in Jerusalem, when he said: "Render therefore unto Caesar the things which are Caesar's; and unto God the things which are God's" (Matt. 22:21). It was with kindly graciousness, therefore, that he could take lodging overnight at Jericho, in the elegant house of the stumpy, dumpy, rich little tax collector, Zacchaeus, whom he inspired to make adequate restitution for moneys unrightfully acquired, and, in addition, to make a large capital gift to the poor (Luke 19:1–10). The fat publican, who had waddled his way to considerable wealth, achieved greater fame through his chance charity than he could possibly have gained otherwise. His entire being had become illumined by coming into contact, however brief, with a spiritual flame. By prescient faith was the blind man Bartimaeus healed, when he met the Rabbi Jesus in Jericho (Mark 10:51). A monastery nests on a mountaintop by Jericho (Fig. 110), founded in the belief that it marks the spot where Jesus resisted the temptation after his baptism (Matt. 4:7–11).

VIII

The Plains of Moab

I

EVERY motion of the artist's brush was followed with rapt attention by the gaping audience. Divinity, strange and striking, was coming to life in the wall-painting. And now the finishing touches were being put to this great fresco, fairly aflame with the hues of the rainbow. Beginning at the left, a large sun cast its effulgence upon a nude god, with seven attendant deities beyond him. In brilliant red and yellow, in startling black and white, these fateful figures were assuming final form. They covered a lime-sur-faced, mud-brick wall, which was thirteen feet long. Already complete was one painting showing a great multicolored eight-pointed star radiantly surrounded by a galaxy of gods fearful to behold, foreign to a mortal world. On yet another wall, in sharp contrast in style, was a painting of a bird, vibrantly alert, done with such naturalistic touch that long ages must elapse before its artistic excellence could again be attained. The brush is still, the artist has stepped back. Overcome by the immensity of his portrayal, he bows his head and intones a prayer. The onlookers join in. The painter is their priest, the walls enclose their shrine, the paintings trace the pattern of their belief in the supernatural.

The faith of these people is firm, the forms of their religion are sometimes frightful. A procession is approaching the shrine with singing and wailing, with ecstatic dancing and declaiming. What objects are those that are carried in its van? A large empty pottery jar, and in the hands of another bearer an infant! Is it silent in slumber or stilled in death? The procession halts in front of the shrine. The priests emerge, the ceremony commences, the child's body is in-serted into this strange receptacle, and the jar is sealed. From whose lips escaped that strangled moan? Such was the gift to the gods of

233

fertility that the earth might yield its riches, the herds bountifully produce their young, the women bear sons in plenty. This sacrifice would serve as a foundation offering. Surely the house reared over it would enjoy the favor of the divine! See how the gods painted on the walls gleam with satisfaction. To them the fruit of the womb that the womb may again become fruitful!

Would you like to visit this shrine and gaze at these deities? It is located in a bustling town of considerable size which stands among green fields in the partly irrigated plain at the northeast end of the Dead Sea. Pay the boatman a fraction of the whole shekel he demands for his services, and have yourself put across the Jordan (Fig. 111), whose flood is surging toward the Dead Sea now clearly in sight. If you have told him your goal, he will set you ashore on the east side of the river, at a point about four and a half miles north of its outlet into the Sea. You will have to go about three miles straight east to reach your destination. There is a salt-encrusted waste to traverse, then up some serried slopes of barren earth where rarely a blade of grass ever grows, before you get to the top of the plain. And then you will have to be nimble, because ever so often you will have to jump across an irrigation ditch several feet broad, whose waters come from the Brook Heshbon. Everywhere you look there seems to be a thriving settlement whose carefully cultivated fields stretch east all the way to the base of the Mountains of Moab. You are in the Plains, or Fields, of Moab.

But you have waited too long! The site you proposed to visit no longer exists, except as an almost unrecognizable ruin, so razed by men and ravished by time that it is barely distinguishable from the uncultivated waste in which it is now set. It is known today as Teleilat Ghassul. Look about you! There are still some irrigated patches in the plain, but no villages, practically no life. To the Jesuit Fathers Alexis Mallon and Robert Koeppel who discovered and excavated this site, we owe our present information about it. The ruins of four towns, the last three being built each on top of the remains of the previously destroyed one, were revealed through their labors, and rescued thus from the oblivion into which they had fallen.

Photo by The Matson Photo Service, Jerusalem

FIG. 111. At Makhadet Hijla, the traditional site of Jesus' baptism, near Jericho, Russian pilgrims in the time of the czars immersed in the Jordan.

First established in the fifth or sixth millennium B.C., in the Neolithic period, the story of the settlements which superseded each other there can be followed by means of their physical remains to the first part of the fourth millennium B.C., well down into the Chalcolithic period.

Fragments of fascinating frescoes, almost modernistic in style, painted on lime surfaces were discovered on the inner side of some of the sun-baked, mud-brick walls of rectangular houses in the next to the last (third) city of the site. Some of the walls had received four or five coats of paint, a new one, apparently, being applied when the previous one had flaked off, or when an impelling religious impulse animated the artist or his patron. Only the fresco with the painting of the lifelike bird had remained comparatively intact when the excavators opened the site. The others were all in greater or less ruin owing to the collapse of all or parts of the walls on which they were painted. Numerous fragments of dramatically painted birds were found, done with primitive forcefulness. The exact nature of these gods, painted and worshiped more than fifty-five hundred years ago, and the character of the religion built up around them remain more or less of an enigma. The main finds, however, indicate a primitive fertility cult.

Five thousand, six thousand, perhaps even seven thousand years ago, irrigation agriculture was practiced in the Plains of Moab and throughout most of the Jordan Valley. That requires considerable skill, long experience, an advanced degree of civilization. Men had to organize to serve their common interest. The equitable use of available water had to be decided in communal council. The lowlands of the Jordan Valley, including the Plains of Moab, were inhabited many hundreds of years, even millenniums, before the rugged, heavily wooded hill country of Transjordan and Palestine was partly cleared and settled. And when, later on, after settlements had sprung up in the hill country, and, on occasion, famine would occur because of lack of rain, then there would be a movement to the lowlands, where perennial streams made the peasants independent of the vagaries of weather. "Now it came to pass, in the days when the judges ruled, that there was a famine in the land. And a certain man of Beth-lehem-judah went to sojourn in the fields of Moab" (Ruth 1:1).

And so the inhabitants of Teleilat Ghassul planted and harvested, stored their surplus grain in moisture-proof clay bins, built houses and shrines, and developed through painful process of experiment the arts of civilization. Many of their utensils were of stone. Mortars, pestles, loom weights, rubbingstones abound—and they spell endless motions of daily toil. Grain had to be ground, skins cleaned, and a host of duties performed, which could be accomplished with tools of flint and stone employed from times immemorial. But the people of Teleilat Ghassul had also learned how to make pottery, well-fired and long-enduring. Indeed, it is of such a distinctive kind that even fragments of it spell for the expert a period of occupation by village dwellers who used much the same wares all over Palestine. Such were their household goods—simple, plain, penurious by some standards, but sufficient for their needs. A man fashioned a house by making mud bricks of rounded or flattened form with his hands, and laying them in place after they had dried in the sun. The women plastered the walls inside and out with a coating of mud, and repaired the flat roof every year or two. Under the thresholds of some of the houses, children were buried in pottery jars. Were such homes not indeed temples? Stone-lined graves were found where the dead were buried with ornaments and pottery vessels, which probably contained food for them in the afterworld. The concern of men with the world beyond is an extremely ancient one.

And then, sometime in the early fourth millennium B.C., Teleilat Ghassul was destroyed—by whom we do not know. It was never again rebuilt. It is probably safe to assume that it was destroyed during some Bedouin raid. Scornful of agriculture, contemptuous of sedentary life, loathing houses and loving their airy and easily movable tents, content with little, bound down by few possessions, the nomads are ever on the alert for an opportunity to break down what they themselves will not build, to purloin the grain of the painful labor of others, to reduce planted fields to unplowed grazing lands, to pitch their tents on mounds which mark the ruins of former towns.

2

I have often met Arabs in the Jordan Valley and in the Plains of Moab who, it seemed to me, were but a step in distance and a moment in time removed from figures familiar to me from the pages of the Old and New Testaments. Such a one was Abdul Selim, who accompanied me on my visit to Teleilat Ghassul and elsewhere in the Plains of Moab. I crossed the Jordan in a small skiff and was met on the other side by Abdul Selim. He was the headman of the small collection of mud-brick houses called Khirbet Sweimeh, located in the Plains of Moab at the northeast end of the Dead Sea. He looked the part of a Biblical character. Tall and lean, serene and dignified, by repute fierce in wrath but just and honest after his fashion, it was obvious that he was a person of parts, however poor his mantle and empty his purse. I could not help telling him the story of Balak, king of Moab, and of Balaam, the soothsayer from Aram, whom Balak had importuned to curse the Bene-Israel encamped in these very Plains of Moab, on the east side of the Jordan, opposite the Plain of Jericho. He was fascinated by the account. "And the Bene-Israel set forward and pitched [their tents] in the Plains of Moab, on this side of the Jordan, facing Jericho. And Balak the son of Zippor saw all that Israel had done to the Amorites. And Moab was sore afraid of the people, because they were many. . . . And Balak . . . was king of the Moabites at that time. He sent messengers therefore unto Balaam the son of Beor . . . to call him, saying, . . . Come now . . . and curse this people" (Num. 22:1–6).

Abdul Selim listened intently and kept on asking if indeed this were written in Sacred Script. When I went on to tell him how, despite the offer of a king's ransom, Balaam refused to curse, but in accordance with God's command uttered words of blessing instead, he nodded his head in complete approval. And when in this connection I told him the story of Balaam's ass, I had to pull out my little pocket Bible and translate for him, amidst numerous "*Ya Allah's*" and "*Allahu akbar's*" on his part, the fascinating tale of the wise little beast. We practically wept together over the way Balaam beat his ass three times because she refused to go forward seeing what Balaam could not see, that the angel of the Lord with drawn sword in hand barred the way. "And the Lord opened the mouth of the ass, and she said unto Balaam, . . . Am I not thine ass, upon which thou hast ridden ever since I was thine unto this day? Was I ever wont to do so unto thee? And he said, Nay. Then the Lord opened the eyes of Balaam, and he saw the angel of the Lord standing in the way, and his sword drawn in his hand: and he bowed down his head, and fell flat on his face. And the angel of the Lord said unto him, Wherefore hast thou smitten thine ass these three times? . . . Unless she had turned from me, surely now also I had slain thee, and saved her alive. And Balaam said unto the angel of the Lord, I have sinned; for I knew not that thou stoodest in the way against me" (Num. 22:28, 30–34). We had almost reached Abdul Selim's little village by that time. And there, standing stubbornly in the little narrow lane leading to it, was an obdurate donkey, heedless of its rider's blows, refusing to go forward. I at least, and I think Abdul Selim too, looked hard up the lane, half expecting to see the angel of the Lord barring the way with his sword drawn in his hand.

3

I had told Abdul Selim that his village of Khirbet Sweimeh bore an ancient name, being the modern Arabic version of the Biblical Beth-jeshimoth, and that indeed most people thought that the adjacent *khirbeh* or ancient ruin represented the remains of the Biblical site. But after I examined it, I had to disabuse him of the idea and extend our search farther until we found the original Biblical site at a place called Tell Azeimeh, located on a commanding position near the foothills of the Mountains of Moab several miles away to the east. Abdul Selim's feelings were somewhat ruffled at this, but he was mollified when I took him with me to the great ruined site of Khirbet Sweimeh and showed him countless fragments of Roman pottery and glass, and explained what an important and thriving place it had been some two thousand years ago, when it was known as Bezemoth. And I told him of the taking of this site together with others in the Plains of Moab by Placidus, one of the generals of Vespasian (shortly thereafter to become emperor of Rome), who had put down a fierce Jewish rebellion with much bloodshed. Josephus reports that Placidus "took Abila, and Julias and Bezemoth, and all [the cities] that lay as far as the lake Asphaltitis" (*The Jewish War*, IV:vii.6), as the Dead Sea was then known.

I described to Abdul Selim how Khirbet Sweimeh had looked in its heyday in Roman times, when more lands than at present were cultivated and irrigated by the waters of the adjacent Wadi Azeimeh and of the powerful spring 'Ain Sweimeh situated about half a mile to the southeast. I told him of the villas and their baths, and the palace that crowned the ancient mound of Khirbet Sweimeh and commanded a clear view of the Dead Sea a little over a mile away. I started to tell him that Roman Bezemoth numbered its inhabitants by the hundreds instead of the poverty-stricken tens in his forlorn little village, that the people of the Plains of Moab could once be counted by the thousands instead of the few hundreds that lived there today, but I desisted for fear of making him feel that his lot was too hard. He wagged his head and stroked his beard and asked if the fragments of pottery and glass at our feet were really as old as I had said they were. I swore "on my head," using an oath familiar to him, that I had spoken the truth. Wonderingly, he put a couple of fragments of pottery and glass in his pocket, thinking no doubt to discuss them with his cronies around the coffeepot that evening.

The original Biblical site of Beth-jeshimoth was located farther east on a hill commanding the outlet of the waters of the Wadi Azeimeh into the Plains of Moab. "And they [the Israelites] camped by the Jordan, from Beth-jeshimoth to Abel-shittim in the Plains of Moab" (Num. 33:49). All the important towns in the Plains of Moab during Biblical times were situated in similarly strong positions. From north to south, in the Plains of Moab, these towns were known in the Bible as Beth-nimrah (to be identified with Tell Bleibil), Abel-shittim (Tell Hammam), Beth-haram (Tell Iktanu), and

Beth-jeshimoth (Tell Azeimeh). They protected, respectively, the strategic points guarding the emergence from the hills of the precious streams of the Wadi Nimrin (known also as the Wadi Sha'ib farther east), the Wadi Kefrein, the Wadi er-Rameh (which, two thirds of the way across the valley, runs into the Wadi Kefrein, and which is known in the hills as the Wadi Hesban), and the Wadi Azeimeh. Such are the modern names of the four streams that traverse the Plains of Moab and such the ancient and modern names of the hill fortresses which in Biblical times guarded their eastern gates.

It was only after the difficult years of pilgrim beginnings were over, and the dangerous centuries had passed when Israelites and Moabites had constantly to be on their guard against enemies from outside and against each other, that these fortified hilltops were abandoned. That occurred in the sixth century B.C. Subsequently, in Hellenistic-Roman times, more expansive sites by the sides of these streams were selected in the very center of the Plains of Moab. They flourished during the beneficent period of peace which prevailed when Rome established political hegemony over broad spaces of the world, and, directly or indirectly, maintained public security throughout her empire. But with the new towns went the old names, along with many of the descendants of the men who dwelt in the old fortresses.

4

The name of Beth-jeshimoth, when transferred to the new site in the plain, became known, as we have seen, as Bezemoth, written in some sources as Bethsimuth or Isimuth. Khirbet Sweimeh is its modern Arabicized version. Similarly, in another instance, the Hellenistic-Roman and later Byzantine and medieval Arabic settlement, called in Greek and Talmudic sources Beth-nambris and Nimrin or Nimri, and called today Tell Nimrin, got its name from the Biblical hill fortress of Beth-nimrah, which is about a mile farther east, and which was abandoned long before the new town was established.

Sometimes this transfer of names from one site to another in the Plains of Moab was complicated by the introduction of a completely foreign one. This occurred in the case of Tell er-Rameh, which is a

conical, ruin-covered hill, located in the south central part of the
Plains of Moab. On and around it in Hellenistic-Roman times a new
settlement was established. It was called Beth-aramphtha or Beth-
ramtha, reflecting the Biblical name of Beth-haram, which had come
to it from the previously occupied hill fortress several miles away,
close to the eastern foothills of the Mountains of Moab. In 4 B.C. it
was burnt down. Herod Antipas rebuilt it on the lavish scale to which
the Herodians were accustomed, and called it Livias in honor of
Augustus' wife. Subsequently the name was changed to Julias, when,
on Augustus' death, Livia was adopted into the Julian gens and
henceforth assumed the name of Julia Augusta. By that time, however, the name of Livias had taken root and it survived till the sixth
century A.D. Nevertheless, the more ancient name never died out
among the native Aramaic-speaking population, so that finally the
comparatively new name of Livias fell into disuse. The old name,
related to Beth-haram, then reappeared, as indicated by the present
Arabic name of the site, Tell er-Rameh.

In another instance, both the original Biblical name of Abel-
shittim and that of Abila, derived from it and applied elsewhere, were
forgotten. It has been possible by means of archaeological finds and
literary materials to identify Abila with Khirbet Kefrein on the north
side of the perennial stream of the Wadi Kefrein, but no trace whatsoever of the name Abila remains today in the Plains of Moab. Indeed, there is not a single place in the Plains of Moab where the
Biblical name still clings in original or even in slightly Arabicized
form as, for instance, at such places as Damieh, Eriha, and Beisan
(Adam or Adamah, Jericho, and Beth-shan) in other parts of the
Jordan Valley.

5

The irrigated and intensively cultivated Plains of Moab formed the
fairest part of the province of Perea. Together with Galilee, it had
fallen to the inheritance of Herod Antipas in accordance with Herod
the Great's last testament, in which he divided his kingdom among
his sons. That was only one of the many times when the lands im-

mediately east and west of the Jordan have been more or less arbitrarily partitioned. Abila and Livias (Julias, Beth-aramphtha) were the seats of the southernmost subsections or toparchies of Perea. In the time of Herod the Great, the toparchy of Livias comprised eighteen villages. These toparchies of Livias and Abila were to be given later by Nero to Agrippa II, having been previously annexed by Rome, together with the rest of the kingdom of his father, Agrippa I, after the latter's death.

In Herod Antipas' days, the territory of Perea stretched along the north half of the east side of the Dead Sea and along the east side of the Jordan River as far as the boundaries of Pella. In other words, it extended between the Arnon, Jabbok, and Jabesh (Wadi Yabis) rivers, and somewhat beyond, taking in the lowlands and part of the hill country to the east. This territory corresponded in considerable part to that claimed for the two tribes of Reuben and Gad in earlier days. Machaerus was the southernmost fortress-town of Perea.

After the Romans, in the year A.D. 72, had finally crushed the hopeless Jewish rebellion against them, they destroyed Machaerus, as well as Herodium near Bethlehem, and the greatest fortress of them all, Masada, overlooking the southwest shore of the Dead Sea. I have walked among the ruins of Machaerus, lost in wonder at the size of the site, and its water supplies secured through reservoirs and cisterns. Once it was a seat of power, short-lived in the record of history. It is remembered chiefly as the place where John the Baptist's head was struck off. Hellenized Jews who worshiped the Lord after a fashion and Hellenized Nabataeans who worshiped a whole pantheon of Greco-Semitic fertility deities, mingled there with proud Romans, to whom both were subject. None of them, however, could lastingly cope with the spiritual strength of Jews like John, whose power came from belief in God.

I have picked up numerous fragments of fine Roman and Nabataean pottery at Machaerus, some of which, indeed, may have been employed at the very banquet where, according to the New Testament, Salome, at the instance of her mother Herodias, solicited and received the unkempt head of John the Baptist (Matt. 14:3-11). An

Arab shepherd stood beside me as I held these sherds in my hands. In answer to his question, I attempted to explain to him that through them I could read the history of a past to which both of us belonged. "And what do they say of the future?" he asked in utter simplicity. And I replied, "*Allah ya'ref*" (Only God knows that).

6

John lived and died for the righteousness of the moral law. Prophetically intolerant of immorality, he was nevertheless possessed of the meekness that characterizes the immortals. When Jesus came "from Galilee to the Jordan unto John, to be baptized of him, John would have hindered him, saying, I have need to be baptized of thee, and comest thou to me? But Jesus answering him said unto him, Suffer it now; for thus it becometh us to fulfill all righteousness" (Matt. 3:13–15). This son of the priest Zacharias (Luke 1:5, 57–63) had done no evil. He had preached the coming of the Kingdom of God. He had urged all who would listen to repent of their sins. He had washed penitents with the waters of the River Jordan in token of their change of heart. But the state suspected that these simple religious teachings had revolutionary implications. So let this rabbi (John 3:26) be beheaded by a Herodian governing with the authority of Rome, and later on, let another rabbi, Akiba, be tortured to death by a representative of the same power for not yielding the right to proclaim and propagate the law of the Lord. "In those days came John the Baptist, preaching in the wilderness of Judaea and saying, Repent ye: for the kingdom of heaven is at hand. For this is that which was spoken of by the prophet Isaiah saying, The voice of one crying in the wilderness: Prepare the way of the Lord, make his paths straight. . . . Then went out to him Jerusalem and all Judaea, and all the region around Jordan, . . . confessing their sins" (Matt. 3:1–3, 5, 6).

The Jordan was central in the life of John, as it was in the life of Jesus, whom he baptized in its waters, and in the life of Elijah, with whom both of them were spiritually linked. To the Jordan they all three repaired at important crises in their lives, seeking solace and inspiration by its banks and in the wastelands near by. John, with "his raiment of camel's hair, and a leathern girdle about his loins, . . . [whose] food was locusts and wild honey" (Matt. 3:4), looked and lived very much as Elijah had, especially during the latter's sojourn in the remote stretches of the Brook Cherith. Indeed, in the popular mind, Elijah, John, and Jesus were frequently confused with each other. When the activities of Jesus were reported, Herod Antipas "was much perplexed, because it was said by some that John had risen from the dead; and by some that Elijah had appeared; and by others that one of the old prophets was risen again. And Herod said, John I beheaded: but who is this, about whom I hear such things? And he sought to see him" (Luke 9:7–9). It remained for Pontius Pilate to be forever pilloried by ordering the crucifixion of Jesus.

7

It was meet that John should have labored beyond Jordan at Beth-abarah (John 1:28) and lived in the land of Perea, and that Jesus should have sojourned there too (John 1:28; Matt. 19:1; Mark 10:1; John 10:40; 3:26), because this was a Jewish land. So much so, in fact, that when the Jews of Galilee wanted to make the pilgrimage to Jerusalem to celebrate the Passover or other festivals there, they chose to take the long roundabout trip through Perea rather than the direct route through pagan and inhospitable Samaria. Had not Jesus, coming from Galilee, when once "he steadfastly set his face to go to Jerusalem" (Luke 9:51–53) been churlishly treated there? The Galileans would ford the Jordan probably near Scythopolis (Beisan), journey southward along the east side of the Jordan Valley to the Plains of Moab, reford the Jordan, crossing over westward to Jericho, halt there for a while, and then continue to Jerusalem. Was not this the very journey that Jesus undertook?

It was while he was beyond Jordan that the rich young man had addressed him: "Good Master, what good thing shall I do, that I may have eternal life?" And Jesus had replied: "Why callest thou me good? There is none good but one, that is God. But if thou wilt enter into life, keep the Commandments. He said unto him, Which?

Jesus said, Thou shalt do no murder, Thou shalt commit no adultery, Thou shalt not steal, Thou shalt not bear false witness, Honor thy father and thy mother, and Thou shalt love thy neighbor as thyself. And the young man said unto him, All these things I have kept from my youth up. What lack I yet? Jesus said unto him, If thou wilt be perfect, go and sell what thou hast, and give it to the poor, and thou shalt have treasure in heaven: and come and follow me. But when the young man heard that saying, he went away sorrowful: for he had great possessions. Then said Jesus unto his disciples, Verily I say unto you, that a rich man shall hardly enter into the kingdom of heaven. And again I say unto you, It is easier for a camel to pass through the eye of a needle, than for a rich man to enter the kingdom of God" (Matt. 19:1, 16–24).

Jesus and John found ready audiences among the people of Perea to whom they could preach. The hard core of the common folk there adhered firmly to the faith of their fathers, though many were attracted to the Hellenistic-Roman way of life with which they came in constant contact. Theirs was a rich land, which, together with Galilee, yielded an income of two hundred talents a year to Herod Antipas. On the whole, they were well governed, even if despotically and at times harshly. In their spiritual life, however, they were directed by their rabbis and not by their rulers, and the masses distinguished sharply between their king and their God.

8

Herod Antipas, usually called Herod in the Gospels, and correctly entitled Herod the tetrarch in Matt. 14:1 and Luke 9:7, ruled over Galilee and Perea for 42 years, from 4 B.C., when his father, Herod the Great, died, to A.D. 39, when he was banished from his dominions by Caligula. What manner of man was this who exercised supreme power of life and death in these two provinces of Galilee and Perea during the entire life span of Jesus and John?

Primarily, it may be said of him that he was a Herodian. They formed a strange and capable family, these Herodians, who were often more Roman than the Romans. Their life stories were swayed more by the stream of the Tiber than by the current of the Jordan, beside which they erected so many imposing edifices. Their aim was ever to please the Caesars whom they served. This they accomplished with brilliant if sycophantic success. When they founded or rebuilt a city or fortress, they very often named it after the reigning emperor or some member of his family. Their motto seems to have been that it always pays to flatter. Herod Antipas was no exception to this rule. We have seen that he founded a city on the shore of the Lake of Galilee and called it Tiberias after the stepson and successor of Augustus, and that he rebuilt Beth-aramphtha in the center of the Plains of Moab and renamed it Livias in honor of Augustus' queen, the mother of Tiberius. His half-brother, Herod Philip, had rebuilt Bethsaida on the north shore of the Lake of Galilee and renamed it Julias in honor of Augustus' daughter, Julia. He had also enlarged and beautified Paneas at the easternmost source of the Jordan and renamed it Caesarea in honor of Augustus. Both Philip and Antipas, like their father Herod the Great, were ardent builders of beautiful cities of Hellenistic architecture.

Herod Antipas was well aware of the fact that he administered his tetrarchy by sufferance of Rome, and that his hold on his dominions hung by the fragile thread of imperial favor, despite the general excellence of his internal rule. He took great pains therefore to cultivate the friendship of his imperial patrons, and for that purpose journeyed frequently to Rome. During one of his visits there he became enamored of Herodias, the wife of his half-brother Herod, an exceptionally unambitious Herodian, who was content to live at ease in Rome, far from the maddening politics of Palestine. That attachment was eventually to prove Antipas' undoing. It resulted immediately in arousing the enmity of his Nabataean neighbor and father-in-law, Aretas IV, whose daughter fled to Machaerus and then escaped to safety in Petra after discovering Herod Antipas' plans to divorce her in order to marry Herodias. Parenthetically it may be stated that this Herod who lived in Rome, and whose name may also have been Philip (Mark 6:17; Matt. 14:3), is not to be confused with the Herod Philip who built Caesarea Philippi and Julias (Bethsaida).

Herodias too, as her name indicates, was a Herodian, and as passionate in the pursuit of her desires as any of her able and unscrupulous relatives. Her first husband, Herod (Philip), was her half-uncle, and by a curious coincidence, so was her second, Herod Antipas. We are told that because of her fury, aroused by the rabbi's rebuke of her shameless remarriage—an abomination according to Jewish law, which forbade a man to marry his brother's wife during his brother's lifetime (Lev. 18:16)—John the Baptist was beheaded. Because of her insatiable appetite for pomp and power, Herod Antipas lost his position. His ignominious downfall was the direct result of her unceasing importunities that he beseech the emperor in Rome for higher rank than tetrarch, to match that of king given to her full brother, Herod Agrippa I. Herod Agrippa had been crowned king by Gaius Caesar, known as Caligula, over the tetrarchy of Batanaea and Trachonitis, which had previously belonged to his uncle, Herod Philip, and which included the cities of Caesarea Philippi and Julias (Bethsaida). It mattered little to Herodias that her husband's tetrarchy of Galilee and Perea was more important and yielded twice the income, although smaller in size than the one her brother had inherited. It galled her into a frenzy of jealousy that her brother should be a king, while she had to remain the spouse of a tetrarch of lower rank. She was determined that her husband too must have a royal diadem placed upon his head, to enable her to appear in public as a queen. So she nagged at Herod Antipas until he went to Rome to beg for a scepter. Agrippa, however, advised of his intentions, and not minded to be outranked by his uncle, even though that uncle had befriended him when he was penniless and without position, managed to reach Caligula's ear first, and implant a false accusation of treason. The result was that Herod Antipas was stripped of all authority and banished to Lyons in Gaul, where, be it said to her credit, Herodias voluntarily joined him in exile. Agrippa thereupon fell heir to Antipas' lands, gradually extending his authority over all the area once ruled by his grandfather, Herod the Great. Herod Antipas, tetrarch of Galilee and Perea, the ablest of Herod the Great's sons, was thus swallowed up in oblivion, but still present

FIG. 112. The Promised Land from Mount Nebo, showing the southern part of the Jordan Valley, the delta of the Jordan extending into the Dead Sea, the Wilderness of Judah, with the towers of Jerusalem and of Bethlehem visible on top of the hills.

in the hearts and minds of men are the teachings of John, whom he killed, and Jesus, whom he sought to see.

9

Like the frame of a harp, the Mountains of Moab enfold the Plains of Moab below them. Protectingly, the hills move forward till they frown down directly upon the Dead Sea. We sat on a height, Abdul Selim and I, with our backs against one of the numerous prehistoric dolmens in the vicinity, and gazed at the watered region extending between the mountains to the east and the river to the west, and I talked about the civilizations that had risen there. Only a few green patches of cultivation showed, although often in the past every acre had been employed. Nearest us, by the first sloping terraces of the mountains, were the ancient fortified hills, some of which had first been settled well over five thousand years ago, and then had been inhabited with interruptions down to the sixth century B.C. Farther west, in the center of the plain, we could make out the later sites established in Hellenistic-Roman times. In these lowlands of the Plains of Moab, Joshua and Moses, John and Jesus, and many others before them, had tarried and left their impress on their time, each man in his own way, each generation after its own fashion. And countless others had watched, as we were watching, the line of the Jordan wending its way to its appointed end.

I thought of Moses standing alone on near-by Mount Nebo, surveying this very scene and looking long at the Promised Land on the west side of the Jordan, which he was fated never to cross. "And Moses went up from the Plains of Moab unto Mount Nebo, to the top of Pisgah, which faces Jericho. And the Lord showed him all the land . . . and the Lord said to him, This is the land, which I have sworn to Abraham, Isaac, and Jacob, saying, To thy seed will I give it. Now I have caused thee to see it with thine eyes, but thou shalt not pass over into it. So Moses, the servant of God, died there in the land of Moab, at the command of the Lord" (Deut. 34:1–5).

The Jungle of the Jordan is at its widest near the crossing before Jericho. Waves of heat make the misshapen grayish-marl hills which

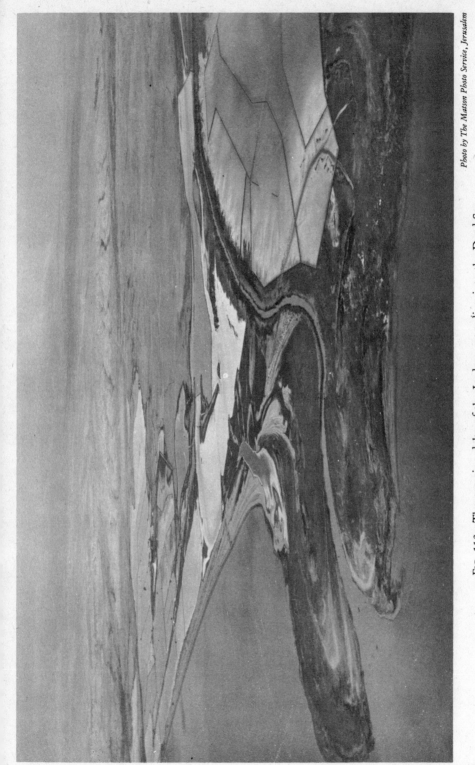

Photo by The Matson Photo Service, Jerusalem

Fig. 113. The growing delta of the Jordan, extending into the Dead Sea.

border it seem to dance a witch's waltz. The glint of the sea and the glare of the bare rock blind the eye. Fantastic rock formations stretch like an evil bar before the green oasis of Jericho, visible beyond them on a higher level. Above the gardens of this "City of Palms" soar the severe mountains of Judah, crowned faintly in the distance by the towers of Jerusalem.

All this, and more too, is what Moses "the man of God" (Ps. 90:1) saw (Fig. 112), as he stood alone on the summit of the mountain—alone, except for the companionship and call of the God whom he had never forsaken, and silent before this manifestation of another of the Lord's miracles. At last, the realization of a generation's striving, the accomplishment of an agony of effort, the fulfillment of driving dreams for freedom! But not for you, O Moses. Your work is done. For you, this is journey's end. The stream of your life is entering into the sea of death.

See how the Jordan builds for itself a curving delta to prolong for yet a forlorn while the length of its course (Fig. 113). There! Its race is run. The muddy river has reached and merged with the lifeless flood of the Dead Sea.

INDEXES

Index to the Text*

*Letters and numbers with dash in between indicate locations on map on inside covers.

255

Index of Biblical Citations